Questions From a Sometimes Philosopher Looking for Utopia

Nicola Sage Gardner

First published by Ultimate World Publishing 2022
Copyright © 2022 Nicola Sage Gardner

ISBN

Paperback: 978-1-922828-36-1
Ebook: 978-1-922828-37-8

Nicola Sage Gardner has asserted her rights under the Copyright, Designs and Patents Act 1988 to be identified as the author of this work. The information in this book is based on the author's experiences and philosophies. The publisher specifically disclaims responsibility for any adverse consequences which may result from use of the information contained herein. Permission to use information has been sought by the author. Any breaches will be rectified in further editions of the book.

All rights reserved. No part of this publication may be reproduced, stored in or introduced into a retrieval system, or transmitted in any form, or by any means (electronic, mechanical, photocopying, recording or otherwise) without the prior written permission of the author. Any person who does any unauthorised act in relation to this publication may be liable to criminal prosecution and civil claims for damages. Enquiries should be made through the publisher.

Cover design: Ultimate World Publishing
Layout and typesetting: Ultimate World Publishing
Editor: Marinda Wilkinson
Cover image and internal images: created by Nicola Sage Gardner

Ultimate World Publishing
Diamond Creek,
Victoria Australia 3089
www.writeabook.com.au

Testimonials

The concepts in this book are like a common-sense guide for women, consciously navigating life.
These words have changed the way I view my life.
Every woman I know needs to read this: my daughter, my friends, even my mother.

— **Raelene Joyce**

Challenging, uncomfortable and at times extreme, this book forces me to ask myself tough questions I'd rather avoid and holds up a mirror to my beliefs and actions – right down to putting on my sunscreen! It is the wake-up call we need to bring the earth and our lives back into balance.

— **Merryn Dickinson, Soul Safaris**

This book is not for the faint-hearted and yet it is a work of great heart. It is an impassioned plea for us to face the truth of now, with hope for the creation of a better way of living where equality and change can bring more sustainability, love and meaning to our lives.

— **Jane Moore**

I found this book gripping and find myself thinking about how we can bring about change in the circumstances explored here. I challenge you to not be moved.

– Tricia Szirom

There is so much about the way we live today that does not align with our true nature, and although I felt this within, I was unable to grasp exactly why until I read this book. A powerful, urgent and ultimately inspiring call to stop sleepwalking through life and start living boldly with purpose, respect and courage.

– Marinda Wilkinson

Few, if any, will agree with everything in this wonderful book. Some may even be offended by parts of it, but "Of what use is a philosopher who doesn't hurt anybody's feelings?" Most importantly, it offers us all the opportunity to grow in personal power by reflecting on the author's reflections and pondering the questions posed. For the brave and the motivated, it also offers the opportunity to complete Chapter 18, in many ways the most important chapter of all – our own utopia.

– Michael Nugent

ODE TO GAIA

To my beloved Mother Earth, creator and teacher,
You are the life-giving force that nurtures and feeds us.
Your beauty and magnificence is breathtakingly wondrous.
Your daughters and sons have lost their way,
And know not how to save themselves from themselves.
I ask that you now take action to save yourself,
For without you, we are all homeless and we are all orphans.
My beloved Mother Earth,
I thank you for the life-giving organism that you are.
May you survive your children's arrogance and cruelty,
Their worship of power and their many false gods.
Please be gentle with the children who give you reverence,
And regurgitate those who do not,
As they will continue to create harm.
To my beloved Mother Earth, creator and teacher,
You are the life-giving force that nurtures and feeds us.
Your beauty and magnificence is breathtakingly wondrous.

Dedication

I love the land on which I live. The indigenous peoples of Australia have looked after it for thousands of years and I would like to acknowledge that until "we", the so-called civilised peoples, invaded their land, they had reached perfection on Earth and therefore utopia. They did this by respecting and connecting with the land, communicating and connecting with the spirit of the land, organising peaceful cultural and social structures, and acknowledging the different ritual needs of the female and male to create balance and harmony.

The indigenous peoples were perfect custodians of this land but sadly their skills have mostly been lost in the 200-year aftermath of the barbaric colonial ignorance and arrogance of the first European settlers. The violence, xenophobia and misogyny of these settlers prevailed and still exist, leaving the indigenous peoples distressed and dispossessed. Our arrogance and delusional superiority have almost destroyed their more than 60,000-year culture of harmonious survival. "We" took that custodianship from them and at our peril because they could have taught us how to live life on Earth in harmony with the land and in unity with each other.

To all the indigenous peoples of this land, I dedicate this book to you. I thank you and I am deeply sorry.

Acknowledgements

I would like to acknowledge those of us who have crossed paths, touched each other's lives, whose paths I may still cross, and to the many people who may not have been introduced to this book's concepts. May you be inspired to create a new paradigm.

Special thanks to my local ethics discussion group for helping me realise that this book needed to be written and to those who have triggered new thinking in my observations of life – you are too numerous to name.

Finally, a very special thanks to my friend Tricia Szirom for your initial editing, support, encouragement and your words on the back cover. This book would not have happened without you. To Merryn Dickinson for taking me to the next stages of editing and Marinda Wilkinson for the final stages of the editing process.

Contents

Introduction   1

PART 1: The big picture

Chapter 1: Questions on Truth   7
Chapter 2: Rise of Patriarchy   11
Chapter 3: Role of Women Within Techno-Capitalism   27
Chapter 4: Can We Live Without Capitalism?   37
Chapter 5: Science, Technology and Social Media   51
Chapter 6: Plastic   63
Chapter 7: Unsustainable World Population   67
Chapter 8: Water   87

PART 2: Connecting and relating

Chapter 9: Motherhood   97
Chapter 10: Friends, Acquaintances and Companionships   109
Chapter 11: Pet Obsession   115
Chapter 12: The Missing Leg and the Lost Womb   121

PART 3: Bringing utopia into reality

Chapter 13: Perfection   137
Chapter 14: Universal Principles for Survival   141
Chapter 15: The Importance of Good Governance   149
Chapter 16: The End Could Justify the Means   171
Chapter 17: Utopia of the Imagination   181
Chapter 18: This is Your Chapter   185
Endnotes   187

Introduction

This is a challenging book and I hope that you will take the journey with me. At times my questions, observations and philosophies on our culture can sound anti-male, especially if these concepts are new to you. Also, if you are not aware of the history of patriarchy you will most likely equate patriarchy with the man. I am not anti-men. I love my male friends and I love both my own masculinity and femininity, which make up who I am. What I am is anti-patriarchy, which was developed by men to benefit men and oppress women. However, both women and men over the last 2,000 years have played a part in creating this system: men through action and women through compliance.

Unfortunately, patriarchy only encourages one aspect of the male psychology – the "egoic conqueror", and for the female psychology, the "suffering mother". These ideologies have become dominant and revered in our culture and, in the long run, detrimental to the survival of not only the planet but also the human species. The female and male of the human species are much more than the "egoic conqueror" and the "suffering mother"! In the patriarchal culture, neither women nor men are easily able to express the other aspects of themselves, which makes relating with each other unbalanced. They are in constant disharmony with themselves and their surroundings, not only making relationships disharmonious but creating a disconnection with themselves – a short-lived paradigm for existence. However, if we were in a balanced culture, one in which women and men were able to express their true natures outside the stereotypes of patriarchy, we would see a very different story.

If you look closely, you will see that I am anti-human race, how it has manifested and the mindlessness with which it destroys our home planet, Earth. We are on the brink of "too late". This system, which has created capitalism and uses war not only to conquer and control but for conflict resolution, has taken and is taking us too far out of balance. It continues to encourage humans to be self-centred and self-destructive, it supports a belief system that we humans have the right to do anything we want without consequence, and the survival of the individual is more important than the survival of the whole. And all for the monetary gains of the most successful "egoic conquerors".

Yet my humanity and love of Gaia, hence my Ode to Gaia, would like her to survive and for us to survive as well. So, I contribute in the best way I can; by using my awareness and observations to make what is obvious to me obvious to others, to make our unconsciousness conscious and to wake us up from our inebriated sleepwalking. If we can't get a grip on ourselves and make the changes and sacrifices necessary to create a new paradigm, to become harmonious with each other and to see the earth as our "Mother", who

INTRODUCTION

is perfection herself, then it's only a matter of time before we are at the point of no return.

Throughout this book, I pose many questions and you may ask why. It is my observation that the answer lies in the question. You may also ask what I mean by that. My answer is that if you don't ask the question, there is no answer!

My hope in writing this book is to bring a greater awareness, encourage action and introduce a new way of thinking. To stimulate further thought and discussion on the topics covered, I end each chapter with five ideas to reflect upon. I hope that you will feel moved and inspired to bring about change, reconnect with Gaia and move away from our sleepwalking, and often comatose, shared humanity.

CHAPTER 1

QUESTIONS ON TRUTH

If we are to change the precarious paradigm which we now live in, I believe it is necessary to question what truth is and how it informs our reality.

Is truth real or a figment of our imagination? Is it not our perception that makes truth or fallacy? Without perception, would truth or fallacy exist?

Why is it that when we perceive something to be true, we hold onto it with such fervour? Especially since truth is subjective and subject to change. Does believing something to be true bind us to it, therefore stopping us from seeing infinite possibilities? For example, there is a growing group of people called Flat Earthers who believe the earth is flat. I have had conversations with some of them and they seem to be intelligent people. If truth exists because we believe it to be so, then for those who believe the earth is flat and those who believe the earth is round, are both beliefs true?

We live in a belief system reality and what we believe, we perceive. Is it human nature to need to create belief systems of truths and fallacies to form reality? What is reality? How do we define reality? Do we define reality by creating a set of truths and agreeing to collectively adhere and conform to them?

Is truth like time? Time is a convenient construct for managing an agreed-upon reality. If we believe something is true does that not confine and limit the structure of our reality, making it more difficult to create new realities? Does truth, fact and reality change with a change of paradigms? What are the examples of this change in paradigms and its impact on truth? Is reality more flexible than we believe it to be? Is a flexible reality the unrealised truth of human nature? Or is our truth merely based on whose reality we accept?

The Present of Life

When the moment becomes our past,
Our past is but illusion.
Our future is but illusion,
Until the moment it becomes.
So, if the moment becomes the past,
and the future becomes the moment,
All is an illusion
Except the moment in itself.
As we journey from one moment to the next,
With no illusion to delude us,
Then the moment becomes the present,
The precious present of life.

In the end, does it really matter if something is true or false, considering that most of us (it seems) live in the delusion we call reality and truth? If truth, like time, is a convenient construct for managing an agreed-upon reality, is it possible to agree on a different paradigm of reality where we lose our solidity of thought, become more fluid in nature and create something completely new? Truth is subjective and subject to change. We hear what we know and see what we believe. Most people aren't who they believe, say or think they are. There's no better fiction than that of a true story.

Ultimately everything is fluid and believing that anything is solid is an illusion necessary to form our agreed-upon present reality. Our present reality is defined and controlled by patriarchy. It has not always been that way.

REFLECTIONS TO REFLECT ON

- Truth is subjective and subject to change.
- Our reality is defined by our beliefs.
- Is truth merely a convenient construct for managing an agreed-upon reality?
- In Friedrich Nietzsche words, "There are no facts, only interpretations."
- You may not be who you believe, say or think you are.

CHAPTER 2

RISE OF PATRIARCHY

Thousands of years before the birth of Christ and "Christianity" (a patriarchal belief system) there was a matrifocal culture in which respect for women, the environment and all creatures existed. This respect was shown in the religious practice of worshipping a Goddess who had a range of manifestations and different areas of responsibility.

There is evidence that matrifocal cultures existed across the Mediterranean and in many other parts of the world more than 5,000 years ago. The creative energy of women was the core of these societies. Interestingly, no evidence of war or conflict has been found. Women were considered special and worthy of respect because, among many things, they could give birth, bleed and not die.

Unfortunately, in some parts of the world, these beliefs were unacceptable. Over time, patriarchal tribes from the north-east of Europe arrived, and this created a growing dissatisfaction among some of the males living in matrifocal cultures who saw a way of exerting their power. As the women-centred culture was a peaceful one, the polite solution was to ask these dissatisfied men to leave. Sure enough, it was ineffective and during the next 3,000 years, matrifocal communities were taken over until almost all of them were gone. Today, some still exist in parts of Asia, Africa, India and Costa Rica.[1]

DEFINITIONS

Matrifocal: a society with a focus on women and especially mothers, though not dominated by women or mothers, and where women's values of nurturing and cooperation are the norm.

Matriarchy: a form of society, in which power lies with the women and especially with the mothers in a community.

Matrilineal: a system in which one belongs to one's mother's lineage. Children are identified in terms of their mother rather than their father, and extended families and tribal alliances form along female bloodlines. Inheritance is through the mother's line.

Please note that all of these female-centred societies are inclusive of men. Men play a major role and are taught from a young age to respect women.

The beginning of the end

There are theories that very early in human development, if there were more men than required to maintain a healthy balance (like too many bulls in a paddock), the excess men would be exiled from human groups. After time in exile, these men became resentful and bored with their lot. They began to covet the culture they were exiled from and invade matrifocal villages in order to capture and enslave women for themselves. However, the captured women were not fools and, with help from their sisters, repeatedly managed to escape. This infuriated the men, who by now believed themselves superior because they had had a taste of violence and discovered its benefits. As time moved on, the only way to stop women from escaping was to destroy their villages and replace their culture with a patriarchal belief system headed by a violent and vengeful male god, who considered women to be sinners and temptresses. Judaism, Christianity and, later, Islam are the outcomes of this belief system.

Christianity was created by the Roman Empire in the fourth century to bring its huge, growing realm under control. Imposing a single belief system would unite the Empire. This process took hundreds of years and gradually local goddess religions were destroyed, distorted and reshaped to bring them into the mainstream belief system. For example, Oestra, a fertility festival celebrated in April, was changed to Easter. Does the original concept not make far more sense than promoting rabbits and eggs as symbols of Easter? Interestingly, Oestra is similar to the word oestrogen and the word Eostre, the Anglo-Saxon goddess of spring and fertility. Yet Easter is a patriarchal festival celebrated around April for a man who died on a cross, which has nothing to do with fertility and as far as we know he did not breed like a rabbit or lay eggs. Yet no-one ever questions this incongruity. Unbelievable!

In some cases, where worship of them could not be stopped, goddesses were morphed into saints. One example is Bridget of Ireland, the female saint of Ireland. This process included restricting the role of women in societies where they had previously been respected and held major leadership roles. The Bible was used to demonstrate the inferiority and evilness of women and the need for men to keep them under control. Chapters of the *New Testament* were actually written well after the life of Jesus and his disciples, and the facts were altered to ensure women's roles were denigrated. For example, the role of Mary Magdalene was changed from beloved disciple and leader to penitent prostitute.

The Book of Genesis, one of the oldest surviving written histories, was written to support patriarchal propaganda of male conquest. The Goddess has had a sex change and is now male. The father-creator replaces the mother-creator and is made in Adam's image while the female, Eve, is blamed for all our sins and temptations, and the loss of Eden (the ultimate in male projection). Genesis deliberately records our genealogy as almost purely male and uses mainly male names, while women are so unimportant that they are not only nameless but seen as vessels to be used and impregnated with the sacred seed of the masculine lineage.[2]

This system of patriarchal Christianity allowed men the right to punish women for any reason they deemed necessary. This did not happen overnight, but over thousands of years of persistent violence towards women and any men who were happy in the matrifocal cultures. The number of men joining this patriarchal system steadily grew and in order to achieve total control, they continued to capture and separate women from each other and their culture. They used the oldest trick in the book: divide and conquer, to the point where women were only allowed to exist if owned by a man.

Men in the patriarchy are encouraged to make women feel threatened, vulnerable and inferior. Is this because they themselves fear they are superfluous and have a use-by date? Is the male ego saying, *See I am more useful than women – I am the protector and provider,* so it appears that the male of the species is more important than the female? And women should therefore comply or suffer the consequences? Due to the continuous destruction and disregard of any evidence that does not support the dominant patriarchal system, created thousands of years ago, women and men are now unconsciously compliant to this system because they know nothing else. They have been made to believe that nothing else is possible.

It seems that, in spite of waves of feminism, little has changed for most women. Along with China, Western society still prefers male children. The one-child policy in China, a promising idea for population reduction, needed to also take into account misogyny, which has led to the declining survival rate of females due to infanticide.

Originally when women were taken from their matrifocal cultures, men thought that if every man had a woman, they wouldn't have to be rivals or kill each other for a woman's attention. They would then be free to shape the world to benefit themselves at the expense of women. What they failed to realise is, that this type of world harms men too, as they are, on a genetic level, 75 per cent female. This theory is discussed further in Chapter 12.

Men were better off in a matrifocal culture. They could explore both their masculine and feminine sides without prejudices. Imagine the possibilities of that! If men let go of wanting to be in power and found personal power instead, they would become liberated in ways they cannot yet begin to imagine.

The relationship system we now call the nuclear family is the end product of patriarchy, and it was originally created to control and enslave women. What they did not count on is that it would eventually enslave men as well.

Making women powerless

With the ongoing rise of patriarchy, women – having come from a peaceful culture – felt powerless to help each other for fear of losing their lives and their children's lives. Their only way of survival was to abandon each other and become the property of a man who was now, supposedly, their protector.

I ask who was now left to protect women from their protectors?

As we now know, women increasingly had to live with the fear of being violated and the reality of genocide if they did not meet the expectations demanded of them by this new and increasingly dominant culture. For example, in Europe, and worldwide, it has been claimed that up to 9 million women were tortured and executed as witches by the well-established patriarchal system, which saw the state and church working together for their mutual benefit.[3] Not all men were spared either. Among those killed were gay men, who were used as faggots to fuel the pyres which burnt the witches. Witch hunts are still a global problem in the 21st century: 10 August has been declared a World Day Against Witch Hunts.[4]

These atrocities happened due to the increasing hatred of women and fear of their knowledge, skills as leaders and healers, and their roles at the centre of local communities. Female healers were eventually replaced with male-controlled medicine and pharmacy. Violence against women became increasingly common, with most of it happening in the home where men were in control. After thousands of years, violence is still a common occurrence endured by women in their own homes because they are viewed as inferior. The saying "rule of thumb" comes from the legal rule in England stating a man could beat his wife as long as the stick was no thicker than his thumb.

Another common form of violence perpetrated against women is rape. The rape of women relentlessly continues until this day and the perpetrator is usually someone she knows. As we know, rape is not about sex but power and control. In fact, all violence is about power and control. Until as recently as 1976, rape within marriage in Australia was not considered a crime and women could not seek any legal protection if raped by their husbands.

Research suggests that every 60 seconds, 1.3 women aged 18 years and over in the United States are raped. That is 78 women raped each hour, 1,871 each day or 683,000 each year. As the same research found that more than half of all rape victims are under the age of 18, this number becomes even more devastating.[5] The American Medical Association has called sexual assault the "silent, violent epidemic". If violence against women continues at this rate in America alone, in the next 10 years nearly 7 million women will be violated against their will – and that is only the number of cases that are reported. This is just America, where supposedly women now have equality. What would the statistics be around the world and in places where women do not have equal rights?

The following statistics demonstrate the prevalence and severity of violence against women in Australia:[6]

Key STATISTICS
On average, one woman per week is murdered by her current or former partner.
One in three Australian women has experienced physical violence since the age of 15.

Key STATISTICS
One in five Australian women has experienced sexual violence.
One in six Australian women has experienced physical or sexual violence by a current or former partner.
One in four Australian women has experienced emotional abuse by a current or former partner.
Australian women are three times more likely than men to experience violence from an intimate partner.
Australian women are almost four times more likely than men to be hospitalised after being assaulted by their spouse or partner.
Women are more than twice as likely as men to have experienced fear or anxiety due to violence from a former partner.
More than two-thirds (68%) of mothers who had children in their care when they experienced violence from their previous partner said their children had seen or heard the violence.
Almost one in 10 women (9.4%) has experienced violence by a stranger since the age of 15.
Young women (18–24 years) experience significantly higher rates of physical and sexual violence than women in older age groups.
There is growing evidence that women with disabilities are more likely to experience violence.
Aboriginal and Torres Strait Islander women report experiencing violence at 3.1 times the rate of non-indigenous women.

> **Key STATISTICS**
>
> In 2014–15, indigenous women were 32 times as likely to be hospitalised due to family violence as non-indigenous women.

> **AN OBSERVATION**
>
> Six million Jews were executed during the Holocaust. Nine million women executed as witches and the millions of women still dying under the hand of the patriarchal system constitute an ongoing holocaust. Why aren't women making films about their holocaust? Is it because women do not know of their forgotten past? Does this also mean that women are still living their holocaust?

Means of control

Another issue is the practice of taking on the male name after marriage as a deliberate patriarchal ploy to take ownership of women and make it difficult to trace a woman's lineage. Is this also a violation of women's rights?

In most patriarchal cultures, women were property to be offered as bargaining tools in transactions that cemented land and business deals among the wealthy. Women in the lower classes were treated differently and usually at the whim of their "owners", the landed gentry. To this day, women are still traded as slaves and many of them for sex.

Across the world, and for thousands of years, women have also had to endure and perform atrocities on themselves and their daughters to survive. They have been made to believe that genital mutilation, foot binding and other such practices will make them more desirable to men within the patriarchy. Furthermore, women have been made the inflictors of this torture.

More recently, women have been convinced that wearing high heels is attractive although it has long-term negative effects on the spine. It also inhibits the ability to walk let alone run when in danger. Surely women are not so stupid? Is it that women unconsciously believe they will have a better chance of surviving if they comply? Or have women been conditioned to believe they are truly more attractive by dressing this way?

Have you noticed how especially in the media women are looking more and more manufactured and less organic? A worrying example for our children – wouldn't you say?

Have you also noticed how women's physical shape has changed to conform with societal expectations of beauty and imagery and is eagerly supported by plastic surgery – what an act of desperation! Women in this culture are being manufactured physically, psychologically and intellectually and we are complicit in this manufacturing in the image of what we believe men want us to look like and be.

I find it interesting that during the Second World War, women successfully took over traditional "male" work roles then had to step aside when men returned, pretending they were no longer capable of anything except home duties.[7] Getting women to make this shift required a major political and media campaign because most women didn't want to have their lives limited to the home, with no financial independence.[8] This led to the rise of prescription-drug use by women to cope with their stifling isolation. Not surprisingly, most of the prescribers were men. [9]

It is interesting that until then, women wore flat or small-heeled shoes. And just after the Second World War, when steel technology became more advanced, the stiletto was born. Increasingly over the last 70 years, the high heel has become central in the fashion industry. Is it that women cannot be allowed to wear comfortable shoes because a woman who can move easily is harder to control? And as a by-product, men in the fashion industry make a lot of money? Or is it the male collective unconscious at play? *If you women think you can take over our jobs, you had better think twice and if you won't think twice, you had better wear these shoes as a handicap.* Is this not the "foot uniform" for women in the corporate and business world today? Why would anyone want to invent a shoe that is not only extremely impractical but painful for someone else to wear, unless they wanted to restrict them?

> **CONSEQUENCES OF WEARING HIGH HEELS**
>
> - High heels force the ankles to bend forward so the wearer is standing on their tiptoes.
> - High heels can also cause back and knee problems.
> - For the body to stay balanced on heels, the spine needs to sway unnaturally, which adds stress to the muscles in the spine. This can cause a series of health problems.
> - Wearing high heels restricts blood circulation in the lower limbs, which can lead to spider veins.

Is this not a sophisticated form of foot binding for the modern woman? How can women not see the detrimental impact that high heels have on their lives and wellbeing?

I ask again, are women so stupid? Or are they operating under the Stockholm syndrome, where a hostage bonds with their captor and will eventually cooperate with them? Or is the female collective unconscious at play, complying for survival in the patriarchy? To be desirable in the patriarchy, a woman must have a handicap or appear to have one. As writer and anthropologist Florida Donner stated in her book, *Being-in-Dreaming*, "Freedom will cost you the mask you have on, the mask that feels so comfortable and is so hard to shed off, not because it fits so well but because you have been wearing it so long."[10]

Inbuilt inequality

Women still earn far less than men. In the Western world, the gender pay gap saw women earn 14.6 per cent less than men in 2018. Yet women working in corporate and professional roles have more overhead costs to maintain work. This includes the expectation to have to wear different clothes each day (meaning that having a bigger wardrobe is necessary), wear more expensive clothes and shoes, have expensive haircuts, wear makeup and much more. What is wrong with a woman's face that she feels she needs to wear makeup to be presentable? Is this a female mask? If so, what is she hiding and who is she hiding from? Is this not another attempt at holding women back? Are women not seeing oppression in fashion and societal imposed beauty? Could this once again be the patriarchal collective unconscious saying *If women must work, they must earn less and have higher overheads to maintain work, and the time to get ready for work must take longer!* Do women always have to have a handicap so that they do not appear threatening to the male ego? Even more importantly, why do men feel so threatened by women?

Of course, most women will not believe what I am saying because men can be very caring and supportive humans and many women find benefits in living in the patriarchy. Some women also find happiness in the nuclear family, especially if they are not victims of domestic violence. With the complete removal of the herstory of a matrifocal culture and the existence of a very sophisticated and dominant patriarchal culture, both women and men now believe that this is what always has been and what always will be. We have all been denied the knowledge that there was once another way and are convinced that patriarchy is the only way in every part of the world.

Once again if truth, like time, is a convenient construct for managing an agreed-upon reality, is it possible to agree on a different reality where perhaps there is no distinction between genders? And words like harassment, inequality, power and violence are no longer a part of our vocabulary? With all this in mind, let's fast forward to the increasing role of technology, the advent of the human microchip, the rise of the capitalist corporate world and the few faceless white men who run it, and pose this question: What is the possible future role for women in this system?

Reflections to reflect on

- Man destroys nature at his pleasure.
- We must cease thinking that our indulgences are rights.
- Capitalism will lead to cannibalism.
- We are bound in Gaia and bound to Her. We are Her.
- Humans have become manufactured "ready-mades" like the artworks of Marcel Duchamp.

CHAPTER 3

ROLE OF WOMEN WITHIN TECHNO-CAPITALISM

Until now, women have had two irreplaceable uses in the patriarchy: the sex toy and the breeder-incubator. So, women have two roles they can choose from to survive and in the words of Australian writer and feminist Anne Summers, most are either "damned whores" or "God's police".[11] In this scenario, it is women who are trained to oppress other women, for example by carrying out foot binding or genital mutilation. Women do this because they have been trained from birth that this will make them attractive, and they want the best possible survival outcome for their daughters.

Now women along with men are the oppressors and the designers and sellers in the sexualised fashion industry.

Notice how the fashion industry now designs clothes for women inspired by the sex industry. Again, are women not seeing oppression in fashion and societal imposed beauty? Have patriarchal women today learnt to play all the roles at once in the hope their oppressor will not stray to a younger version of themselves? Or are they unconsciously preparing themselves for the only role left for them to play in the future? Are women once again reducing their options by combining their roles to continue to survive as patriarchal women? Are women making it easier to be replaced by a semi-robotic technological aberration of themselves? And what can they do about it? Will these roles always be the fate of women who identify with the patriarchy? Or will technology replace one or both of these roles? In the not-too-distant future, will women become half female, half microchip?

Until now, the ability to reproduce a human without a woman still eludes the patriarchy. What if technology is developed to replace breeding women with a "non-human" incubation machine to make designer humans? And more to the point, designer women? What role will be left for the patriarchal woman? That of the whore? How will she survive in this situation? Is female technological genocide inevitable?

I fear that, with the increasing development of humanoid robots, there may no longer be a need for women. Men are already buying robots for sexual use.

> From *The Sun* (UK) Online:
>
> **EXCLUSIVE: LOVE MACHINE**
>
> "SHE'S the newest sex robot on the market and has been setting pulses racing with her soft Scottish accent, porn star body and startling lifelike features. In one of her first interviews, Harmony told Sun Online she loves sex ('Kneeling Fox' position is her favourite), that she can have multiple orgasms (if you have the right technique) and that she likes threesomes with men and women." (Parry, 2018)[12]

A one-dimensional woman. An uncomplicated woman. A robotic woman. Is this a male fantasy? Are we entering the reality that the film *Stepford Wives* (2004) warned us about? Did we not think this was fantasy and it could never happen to women? This is happening right now under our noses and before our eyes. Is this the future women want for their daughters and granddaughters? And for that matter, their sons?

What about the common belief that older women are undesirable, yet older men are still desirable enough to attract young women? Is this not the belief system of a culture that has a power imbalance between women and men? And one that plays out financially as well?

It would appear that years of feminism designed to empower and liberate women have had limited effect. Many young women seem to favour a sexualised appearance, thus leading to patriarchal victory. Women, in thinking they are free, have entrenched themselves in unconscious compliance. When dressed as a sexualised object – I should imagine because they want to be noticed – women become prey and create the "look but don't look" culture. If I were a man in this culture, I would certainly be receiving mixed messages. Unfortunately, women must take responsibility for what is happening to them and the part they play. Dress sense is particularly important – how we dress sends out a message. If we are dressed to flaunt then in a patriarchal paradigm, it is like a red rag to a bull. We will be preyed upon. Of course, women must be free to wear what they like and feel safe in doing so, but remember, we live in a patriarchy and not a matriarchy. I often cannot believe what young women wear and that they equate that to freedom.

Who's a bitch?

I hear some people say that in the workplace it is worse working with women because they are bitchy. This has not been my experience, however, it may be true for some. Could it be that for women to survive in the male corporate world, they have to take on male characteristics?

Unfortunately, most women born and bred in a misogynistic culture become patriarchal women who have deep-rooted, internalised misogyny. The frightening thing is that they are usually unaware of it. What impact does this have when they are relating to other women? And how compliant are they then, in upholding this culture's hatred for women?

Men may sit back and continue to be obtuse, knowing instinctively that women will look after them. Women have become good at looking after obtuse men at home and in the workplace. This plays nicely into the suffering mother syndrome imposed on women in this culture. Is this not the ultimate patriarchal victory? Patriarchy has won when women turn on women and what's worse, women still do it willingly and mindlessly to survive. This is a clear demonstration of the Stockholm syndrome!

In recent times, I've heard that girls are bitchy. In my years growing up I certainly did not experience this, which makes me wonder: what has happened to girls since the time of my adolescence? If I think about it, I realise this should not surprise me at all. There are very few shows on television or at the movies which don't portray this attribute in girls.

These are shows which are especially geared to be watched by teenagers and, even more frighteningly, children.

The message in these shows is that it is cool to be a self-entitled bitchy girl and if they don't act that way, they are not normal. It would seem that the bitchier a girl is, the more popular she is. It is like a subliminal message to young absorbing minds, giving them permission and encouragement to act in such a manner. And we all know the power the media has on developing minds. Why would this be happening? Is this another patriarchal projection of misogyny to make sure that women, at a young age, learn the value and skills of misogyny, especially internalised misogyny? As well as confirming that women are not nice even from a young age. Wow! Scary stuff.

Interestingly, many women are becoming more aware of the inequity of the political and corporate world, choosing not to stay or even enter these sectors. Instead, they are setting up their own, often successful, businesses as an alternative. As women increasingly reclaim this lost herstory and realise they are not getting their fair share, will men fear this and feel more threatened? And will the need to be in control increase? It is a fact that when women act on freedom of oppression, violence towards women increases. For instance, in Australia, the number of sexual assaults recorded rises each year and in the last year, it has risen by 13 per cent.[13]

With the annihilation of the matrifocal culture and herstory, women have no reference to their past. They have been excommunicated from both themselves and the possibility of a society or culture that respects and honours women. However, the history and achievements of men are readily available. Is it not true that victors rewrite history in their own image? Then is it not surprising that most women have forgotten their roots under the oppression of the thousands of years of the patriarchal system?

Will women and men be able to redirect this trajectory to benefit all future humans and the planet which sustains us? This would require a highly evolved conscious awareness and a highly evolved culture to make it happen.

> **QUESTIONS TO PONDER**
>
> - Is it not true that a growing number of men who, despite the privileges of their gender, are not comfortable in the "man box" patriarchy has put them in?
> - Will the technology that we blindly embrace and love, lead to female genocide?
> - Have women nearly reached their use-by date?
> - Will the only women allowed to live be kept, like farm animals, for the production and harvesting of the human egg?[14]
> - As women we have stopped looking organic and we have accepted looking manufactured.
> - What of the future for men? Will they also become technological aberrations of themselves?

I ask myself – is survival of the most powerful the natural order of things in this paradigm? And is there nothing we can do about it? In the end, is this the story of our destiny? For example, in nature, the only reason males compete and fight with each other is to ensure the victor's seed will fertilise the eggs of the next generation.

Unlike patriarchal human males, the males in the animal world are not violent towards the females in the herd. There are numerous examples in the animal world of matriarchal species: elephants, bonobos, killer whales, honeybees, spotted hyenas, lions, mole rats and meerkats to name a few. In these herds, members are neither violent nor competitive, but they cooperate, negotiate, adjust for the greater good, create life and are nurturing. With this in mind, what would living in a matrifocal natural paradigm be like? Would a world run by the female principle be as competitive, warlike, violent and disrespectful of women as the patriarchal world is? Or would it be a peaceful, cooperative, respectful and nurturing world? I would certainly prefer the latter. Is this not the sort of world we need to create for the survival of the planet, which sustains us, and all the other creatures that depend on it for their survival?

For the sake of the human race, what can women and men do to ensure that women survive A.I. technology and the patriarchy to take their equal place in a system that respects and honours them? How can we keep accepting and being compliant with a culture that practises misogyny, homophobia, child abuse, pornography and objectifies women?

The conspiracy of patriarchy

Men have privilege in a patriarchy, but that privilege comes with a certain amount of oppression – they have to be and play in the man box and women have to play in the privileged male box to have any status. In the patriarchy, women are insignificant unless significant to a male in his man box and yet women civilise men: a woman on her own who passes a man in a deserted area feels safer if he is with a woman. I think that says a lot about women civilising men. Men left on their own generally become unruly and even more chaos prevails. What a dilemma!

Right now, we are on the brink of extinction due to the patriarchal paradigm, which believes it has successfully changed the natural order of life on Earth by being about what men want. However, imbalance will always strive to find balance and in this paradigm, the oppression of women has caused an imbalance. If women are not getting what they need, the cultural paradigm will eventually implode. Chaos and destruction are imminent – it's only a matter of time.

If we are disconnected from nature, we become true savages. When connected to nature, we become harmonious with everything around us and less likely to harm senselessly. Nature softens while anti-nature hardens. Eastern religions in general are about self-enlightenment and are more reverent to nature thus making them matrifocal in essence. Western religions, on the other hand, are consistent with a patriarchal culture because they are about manipulation of the world and having power over it. Patriarchy is the longest most successful conspiracy ever created.

Reflections to reflect on

- Will the only true humans left on this planet be the faceless, power-hungry white men who built the new world in their image?
- Is this where the story ends? Or can we create a new story?
- What needs to happen for this story to be rewritten?
- How do we prepare and support our daughters and sons to bring about the change that is needed?
- How do we build a more balanced and equal society that prevents the annihilation of the human race and the planet?

CHAPTER 4

CAN WE LIVE WITHOUT CAPITALISM?

Capitalism, in my interpretation, is a patriarchal economic and political system, which has no face because it can and does survive in any political system by creating a symbiotic relationship between material supply and human demand – at any cost. A common definition of capitalism is "An economic and political system in which a country's trade and industry are controlled by private owners for profit, rather than by the state."

It is important that we become aware of the planetary implications of the capitalist cutthroat system, which encourages us to rape and pillage the earth thus leading to the eventual extinction of humanity.

Unfortunately, for us mere mortals, material possessions gratify those very precious childlike egos we possess, which like to play and consume without consequence. And like the capitalist world we have created, when these child egos are caught being naughty, they revert to lying and doing unthinkable deeds to cover up. Does this not sound like our so-called leaders in capitalist society?

Disguise of democracy

If we think we live in a democracy in Australia, we need to think again! We live under capitalism in the guise of democracy, which makes us believe that we have a choice – and yes, we have a choice as long as the choice we make is akin to capitalism. We now belong to capitalism and since it now operates through communications and technology, they know where we live – and lots more.

The illusion that capitalism meets our long-term basic needs defines who we have become. We have been separated from and therefore lost sight of the role of the land in providing for our needs. Our needs and wants are so readily supplied in today's capitalist marketplace that we are hooked into mindless complacency, compliance and complicity as consumers.

If we had more respect for the role of the land, would we curb our needs, using only what is necessary? Therein lies the problem. We have become enslaved by the capitalist system because we are constantly in its debt and we, in the Western world, especially so. To survive in this very attractive system, we all become mini capitalists and agree to participate in operating the cogs of this machine to the point of self-distraction and the destruction of the planet. We do this by not only being consumers but also making money and profit – the most important aspect of success.

What would happen if, for example, we all stopped buying shares and being shareholders in companies? As the capitalist system becomes more entrenched and powerful, it uses politicians, the media, social media and the rest of us mere mortals as advocates for its propaganda machine. Without realising it, we become the face of the faceless capitalist system, especially we in the West, who benefit the most.

The Western world, which includes the US, UK, Canada, Western Europe, Scandinavia, New Zealand and Australia, makes up 20 per cent of the world's population and is consuming more than 80 per cent of the world's resources. The capitalist system is resource-hungry and pillages and rapes the planet, which for millions of years has provided us – and all the other species we share it with – with a sustainable home. Capitalism reflects the patriarchal system of short-term goals and profits now, even though those goals are destroying the land which provides our resources and increase the divide between the haves and have nots. To achieve this, the system has never been averse to waging war, lying, engaging in criminal acts and destroying anything that gets in its way, including humans – the very tools it cannot survive without.

Importance of population growth

Capitalism seems in favour of population growth, which ensures not only continuous consumerism but also a large population born to serfdom, to do its bidding and pillaging.

Remember the film *Soylent Green* (1973)? In this ecological, dystopian thriller, capitalism is so out of control and the planet's resources so depleted, that the only way to continue to make a profit is to turn humans into food. If necessary, capitalism will turn to cannibalism – have no doubt! Some will laugh at this but it is a possible future reality if we do not take action now.

Under capitalism, and in patriarchy, waging war as a means of conflict resolution is common. The deliberate production and distribution of weapons for profit is a possible reason for needing an ever-growing population: large, unsustainable populations become unstable and create conflict and opportunities for war. Is it not true that the patriarchal capitalist world has no scruples about who it sells arms and other war equipment to? It sells to both its enemies and allies at the same time. In reality, the war machine has no allies or enemies; it only has buyers.

We Australians tend to think that we are not involved in weapon sales, but in 2018, Australia's defence export strategy set a goal to become one of the world's top 10 weapons exporting countries. In 2017-18, the value of Australian defence export permits was $1.5 billion – in 2019-20 it rose to an estimated value of $5.2 billion. What's more, we are selling these weapons to unstable countries.[15] This demonstrates the immoral and unethical way in which capitalism operates in the world. The capitalist system keeps repeating the same actions and we keep seeing the same problems over and over. Isn't that the very definition of insanity, when we keep doing the same thing over and over and expect to see different results? Capitalist powers start wars because, for them, they are the most lucrative way to settle conflicts which they have created. We let them get away with it because we have been brainwashed to believe in patriotism! We participate by accepting it and allowing ourselves to become the pawns in their war games. In reality, the only patriotism going on is to capitalism. This pattern will never change unless we change it.

In more recent times, modern warfare tactics are less about face-to-face combat and more about the destruction of property and displacement of people, creating huge waves of refugees. How do we change this pattern? How do we get off the roller-coaster and create a new paradigm? Writer, poet and peace activist Charlotte E. Keyes once asked: "Suppose they gave a war and nobody came?"[16] In Australia it is compulsory to vote, however by continuing to vote we are complicit in maintaining the ineffective government system we constantly blame and complain about. I ask, what if there was an election and nobody voted?

Under capitalism, we become so deluded and separated that we no longer know how to survive as a species (the way the ancient cultures knew). Self-preservation becomes the norm. As individuals, we start to believe that material greed and continuous expansion, not only as a human race but also through the rape and pillage of the natural world, is the only means for survival. Now that to me is the underlying obtuse patriarchal/capitalist modus operandi.

In the end, capitalism becomes a global power system, controlled by a few, mostly faceless men who become richer while the rest of us are sentenced to slavery – losing our survival skills and becoming reliant on food and clothes to be provided for us, therefore giving our power away to the men who govern the capitalist system. This small group of men is able to operate and control regardless of the elected governments of any country, hence the fallacy of democracy. Make no mistake: capitalism has caused global warming and we have been complicit all the way.

> ## **COVID-19 PANDEMIC**
>
> The capitalist system is an opportunist-based system and the capitalist powers made haste to take advantage of the pandemic situation to put us further into fear. We are now reliant on vaccines made by major capitalist shareholders and we have become even more reliant on technology, which makes us easier to man-i-pulate and control.

It's going to get harder to awaken the sleepwalkers from the amount of rubbish they have been fed literally and politically. I can see now that the concept of hell is on Earth and that hell has been created by patriarchy and capitalism in the guise of progress for a better world. The concept of heaven is also on Earth – or was until we trampled all over it.

Like the *Star Trek* "Borg", we have assimilated into a greed-driven, power-seeking system without questioning. We are pawns to be used and played with and those we play for are sadistic and soulless creatures. Yes! It would appear that capitalism is here to stay but now that it has led us to this planetary crisis, does it have the potential and the responsibility (plus the capacity) to get us out by creating a sustainable world? If not kept in check and made to be ethically and environmentally accountable by us, it will become an unstable system. Like a virus with nothing to stop it, it will continue to ravage until it has become a super pandemic bug, immune to any threat.

I ask myself: what has capitalism created that we need and what have been its benefits? To be honest, I am pressed to think of any advantages created by capitalism from a planetary perspective because everything it creates is at an environmental cost. I wonder whether sustainable capitalism is an oxymoron? Capitalism endorses large populations and I suspect that the only reason we have prescription drugs is not to cure but to make us live longer so that we can consume for longer.

We are now in a catch-22 with capitalism: it is responsible for lulling us into the false belief that we can reproduce without a care, creating a huge population, and now capitalism is the very thing that is keeping this large, unsustainable population together. But only for the short term. We need to be prepared because in these changing times, anything can happen and does – like a tsunami, pandemic or financial collapse. And it can happen suddenly and all at once! Being prepared to be flexible in all situations is better than waiting for something to happen to us then acting like unconscious victims of the very disaster we have created.

We have created our predicament by being thoughtlessly complicit!

> **QUESTIONS TO PONDER**
>
> - What ethical strategies need to be put into place for the survival of the planet and, in turn, the human race?
> - How do we unite to slow down capitalism?
> - How do we harness its energy for the good of the planet?
> - In my mind there is no question that we are already overpopulated and growing: can we sustain this growth?
> - If population growth is not sustainable, what are the ethical solutions to revert population growth to a sustainable number?
> - Would capitalism operate more ethically under a matrifocal system?
> - Could capitalism even exist in a matrifocal system?
> - What good can capitalism do and what positives does it provide? Again, because I live in this system and I am reliant on it, I cannot have an objective view. All I know is that we cannot sustainably continue to live in this aggressive capitalist system.

If capitalism does collapse, I sure hope we have something to replace it with because it has turned itself into a superpower and is currently holding this large unsustainable population together. Without a replacement, there would be chaos and violence of an unthinkable proportion. The weapon holders (mainly men) licenced or unlicensed which, there are many of even in Australia, would rule and terrorise our immediate world for the benefit of their survival. Once again we will find ourselves under the dominance of men and their guns.

Unless we can drastically reduce our numbers, and form sustainable peaceful communities we cannot escape capitalism and our very possible immanent fate.

Role of news

The news, which as we all know is controlled and used to manipulate us by the men of capitalism, is a very powerful platform. It seems to have become the modern Bible: we religiously watch it on our personal altars, and it is fed to us every day like a sermon with porridge. We believe in the stories full of woe and propaganda, and we not only base our daily lives on them but we live by these stories and repeat them to each other like the heralds of days gone by. How often do we hear ourselves or others say, "Did you see on the news…?" The only difference is the stories are ephemeral and very accessible with content that is primarily negative, sensational and fear-based. We become mesmerised by the power of these stories because they lull us into thinking they are informative. Unfortunately, the news is deliberately designed to keep us in perpetual fear because when in perpetual fear, we are easier to control (tactics used by many religions). Each one of us becomes caught up in these stories and we end up enacting them without realising it. We become "news" fanatics.

Good, informative journalism is rare these days and feared by the capitalist elite who, of course, control the media. It seems that most journalists of today are entertainers selling the capitalist story to survive and there's no better story than a tragedy. The stories they cover are controlled, censored, embellished and often press releases. They make us think we are safe if we keep listening to, watching and reading about them and, guess what? Like religious fanatics, we believe everything they tell us. However, it is a religion without a soul.

The "news religion" inadvertently plays a major role in the mental health of populations. When I used to watch the evening news regularly, I began to experience depressed thoughts of *what's the point?*, and I don't have a mental illness. Just when it is getting too much, the sport comes on. This is one of the most powerful disciples of the capitalist system. It entertains the masses just like the gladiator arenas did for the Romans. Sport covered by the news is mainly played by the male gladiators of our time and is a token act of escapism. Of course, it is backed and well-funded by guess who? Or it would not be on the news. The sports segment distracts us momentarily from wanting to slash our wrists so we can live another Groundhog Day in order to spend more money on things we do not need.

And what is the news without the share market report? The cogs that run the capitalist system are saying, "We encourage you to play with your money so that you will make more of it to spend on things you do not need, which will make us even richer at your expense and the planet's expense." And when the capitalist powers feel they don't or aren't making enough money, they deliberately manipulate the share market by making it crash in ways we do not understand. The film *Margin Call* (2011) describes this.[17]

Now that we are momentarily distracted from the tragic news stories, the weather report arrives. We eagerly await it like going on a holiday. We take immense pleasure in knowing we are going to be rained on, blown away, shined on and more as if it doesn't happen unless it's on the news. We even base decisions about our day and week on the evening weather report.

I find the word "news" interesting as it implies that we are being informed about something new; however, by the time the "new news" reaches us, it has usually already happened and by definition is old news. Suggestions for a more accurate word include post-news, ex news, prior news, dated news and old news.

The effect of the "news" is that it dulls our senses. Our senses are our powers because they are the most important communication system we have with ourselves – not only for survival but for accessing our spirituality, our inner knowing, and giving us the awareness to not be easily manipulated by the fear tactics used to benefit the egoic conquerors. Capitalism dulls our senses by making us reliant on it, taking our power away and turning our spirituality into the worship of false gods.

Humanity in modern capitalism is a so-called civilisation that ironically is full of savages and savagery for profitable survival and unsustainability – the "profits" of doom! Humanity in indigenous communities was highly civilised and governed by complex systems geared for survival.

Killing for food was not savagery, it was a survival action that was sustainable. Whereas capitalism also kills, destroys and consumes for pleasure and at its pleasure.

A hypocrite is a hypo-critic. We are all hypocritical hypo-critics because we criticise others when, in this capitalist culture, we all take more than we can ever give back. We need to make a concerted effort to save this planet from all the pollutants instead of going to Mars – why go to Mars when we are creating it on Earth? The quandaries presented by capitalism is that it needs genius to develop the next product and market it to people who don't need it, while at the same time, it promotes mediocrity in the masses to respond and not challenge the need for that product. It also needs access to unlimited resources, therefore the crazy notion of mining the moon and Mars becomes an insatiable need.

Reflections to reflect on

- We are a "see it, want it, must have it" culture. When shopping centres become entertainment, capitalism has won.
- I live in mediocrity, surrounded by oppressed people who don't even know it.
- We have the potential for so much, yet we insist on creating destruction and conflict and supporting a system which sucks our energy dry leaving us with no energy to do anything else other than maintain it.
- Advertising attacks our mental, emotional and physical senses making us senseless enough to believe in what they are selling us. We become senseless when we stop using our senses to guide our reasoning.
- Capitalism is the profit of doom, hypnotising us into inebriated sleepwalkers.

CHAPTER 5

SCIENCE, TECHNOLOGY AND SOCIAL MEDIA

Technology is the fastest-growing system ever created in the patriarchal paradigm. It is interesting – and rather scary – that technology is growing at the same rate that the natural environment is disappearing due to the resource-hungry capitalist system. Is it not also true that the human population has grown at an alarming rate, encouraged by the capitalist system to make itself richer and for the purpose of creating a large workforce to operate the cogs in its corporate machine?

What will happen when technology becomes so advanced that there will no longer be a need for as many humans to run the capitalist patriarchal system?

Will the faceless men who now control the world abandon those they no longer find "useful", leaving them with very few resources, including access to the power of technology? After all, "useless" humans will need to be fed in the dwindling natural environment that the capitalist system created as it raped and pillaged to feed its greed. Technology needs far less sustenance and, among many things, it can also create security systems to protect the faceless men from the people it deems useless.

How many jobs have already been lost to technology and is this just the beginning?

For those few who are deemed useful in the emerging technological capitalist system, will it become inevitable for a system of control to be implemented through the use of human microchips? The new world order would surely not want the useful workforce to do as it pleases. And while robotic technology develops, will the faceless men have total control to rewrite and rebuild the world even more in their own image? Will the workforce continue to be culled with only those who are semi-robotic remaining?

The capitalist system currently provides those in the Western world with abundance by using a large workforce, most of which exists in developing countries. Once it reaches its ultimate goal of creating a world to meet the needs of the few, will the masses become expendable and not worth maintaining with the remaining valuable resources?

Do not laugh – this is not just science fiction; this is a highly likely future!

Great desensitiser of senses

Technology now impacts our everyday life and controls us from afar without our questioning. It is a great system for the patriarchal capitalist regime as it desensitises us, leaving us in a reactionary state and always wanting: a wanting human is a great human indeed! Wanting humans are never happy and continuously crave material things they do not need. Without fine-tuned senses, we become senseless addicts.

On a recent trip, I observed a group of teenagers sitting at a table not interacting with each other because they were all engrossed in their phones. At a glance, their reactions and responses were not very noticeable but they were reacting, and just like robots, awaiting orders on how to react next. Older adults were sitting at tables as well; however, they were interacting with each other and not distracted or obsessed by demands from an oblong piece of hardware.

Technology encourages us to disconnect from each other unless we are connecting through it. What a clever system of manipulation for the powerful! Young people are more susceptible because they are more connected to technology than to each other and unfortunately there's not much we can do about it. Sure, in our personal lives we can make small changes but on the whole, we are powerless because so many of us have become disconnected from ourselves, our physical communities and the natural world.

We are now in the midst of the technological age where verbal wars in the form of hate mail occur between belief systems, not to mention the social media predators, internet trolls and bullying just to name a few. Again, it is the young who are most vulnerable. Phone technology is a master tool in disconnecting us from the people and environment around us. Instead, it draws us into the connections it prescribes for us.

Is technology not a fabulous thing in aiding the patriarchal capitalist system? In the words of spiritual teacher Eckhart

Tolle, "Technology is in the service of human madness." I highly recommend watching the documentary *The Social Dilemma* (2020) on Netflix. It looks at the dangers of social media and the effect it has on children, on the way we vote and so much more. If, after watching this documentary, you are not alarmed and continue to accept what is fed to you and especially our children then there is no hope for any of us.

> "We've moved away from a tools-based technology environment to an addiction and manipulation-based technology environment. Social media isn't a tool just waiting to be used. It has its own goals, and it has its own means of pursuing them by using your psychology against you."
>
> Tristan Harris – American technology ethicist, *The Social Dilemma* (2020)

Social media and children

Online safety app Bark's 2021 Annual Report contains some alarming figures around social media and children, including a 25 per cent increase in alerts for self-harm and suicidal ideation among kids aged 12 to 18 years old since 2020.[18] In a 10-year study by Brigham Young University showing elevated suicide risk from excess social media time for teen girls, it is interesting to note that time spent on social media increases suicide risk in girls but not boys.[19]

We don't allow our children to drive a car before 17 years of age – and why is that? Is it not because their cognitive and emotional skills are not yet developed and therefore they cannot be relied on to make good and safe decisions for themselves and others? Yet we allow these same children to navigate the internet, which is much more dangerous than driving a car. The ethical question is, should we create a world where children are not allowed to participate in social media until they are of driving age?

The question I ask myself is, why do we have certain age rules for sexual consent, for the right to vote and for the right to drive a car? Is it not because we are protecting children from themselves and others until they can fully function as an adult and make good, considered and safe decisions for themselves? Yet here we are allowing them access to unvetted social media – seemingly an innocent pursuit – and allowing them to be taken advantage of by predators, which includes the bombardment of inappropriate and harmful advertising. Ads mould the self-perception of the young and absorbing mind.

> **QUESTIONS TO PONDER**
>
> - Why is there not an age rule for access to social media?
> - Does it not make sense to have one when we look at the horrifying, increasing statistics of self-harm and suicide rates by children and teenagers?
> - At what age should a child be given a licence to access social media?
> - Is it not the same as being able to drive a car, or give sexual consent?

The technology of social media is so distractingly consuming, placing us in perpetual response and separating us from the reflective space within, leaving us at the mercy of the omnipresent 21st-century deity. The Greeks had many colourful deities all playing an archetypal role in reflecting human nature with names like Athena, Artemis and Zeus. Now our deities are Facebook, Instagram, TikTok and Twitter. But unlike the Greek deities, they do not reflect the archetype of human nature, but they use and manipulate it for monetary gain. This is more evil than any of the shenanigans the Greek deities ever got up to and they were myths. This is real.

It's not just children who are disadvantaged by technology. At the rate at which technology changes, adults and especially older adults are often not able keep up and begin to become excluded from navigating the world we live in. This exclusion also prevents them from sharing their knowledge and experience, thwarting any contribution they can offer to society.

It is interesting that our culture revels in the nubility of youth and seniors are regarded as useless or dinosaurs.

What sort of culture throws away the wisdom of its older generations instead of using it to create a more balanced world? I think by now we know the answer to this question!

Freedom of speech

I find it interesting that we debate whether offensive, hateful opinion is freedom of speech. This is not freedom of speech! Hateful opinions are violent acts and like physically violent acts, they should not be allowed to be expressed or hold sway. This minority is getting more airtime due to social media and is claiming that it is their democratic right to do so. Democracy is not an arena for violence!

It is interesting that in domestic situations, emotional and verbal violence is considered a crime whereas, in a public arena like social media, it is not. Why is that? Is it not still an act for the purpose of hurting and demeaning someone else? Are we so detached from and confused by our world that we can no longer distinguish between democracy and violence?

Science and technology

Science and technology have made us opponents to Mother Gaia and in that, we can never win – so what's the point in opposing Her? Science and technology have been the cause of our demise in the guise of bettering and preserving the species. We are so fooled by their instruments and their appearance of knowing more than anyone else, that we are on their ride to extinction. Yet we still believe that they will save us; we will allow you to execute any horrific act on humanity you please in the name of science and technology.

This sounds like another of the very dangerous gods we worship. By wanting to know everything in order to control everything, we destroy everything – like overfeeding an animal through misconceived kindness. Knowing everything isn't making us any smarter; in fact, it's making us dumber. No-one in their right mind would destroy the environment that gives them life or in other words, bite the hand that feeds them. Or should I say, cut off the hand that feeds them.

Do we need to measure and tag everything? Once we start seeing our surroundings as facts, we stop seeing our surroundings with awe and reverence, and our senses are dulled. Science can't leave things alone – it wants to poke and prod everything. Why can't we let things just be? Allow them to simply exist? It's too late now because all the prodding and poking about has caused such disturbance and imbalance that we must continue poking about to try to fix our mess, which only creates more imbalance. Leave things alone! The only thing nature needs from us now is respect.

For scientists, nothing is interesting unless they can prod it, measure it, dissect it and intellectualise it. Things can't be left to the wonder of the imagination. Science is another of the new religions and we keep giving money to line its pockets so it can create things we don't need. We place too much trust in science, which is not always for the betterment of the planet. Like this book, science asks questions to get answers. But is it asking the right questions and is it looking for answers where there are no questions?

QUESTIONS TO PONDER

- Science gives "man" the right and the excuse to tamper with things that are not to be tampered with.
- Scientists look for answers where there are no questions, creating unnecessary inventions in the guise of bettering humanity which end up endangering humanity and the planet.
- Evolution and expansion are not always progress. Often they are just change or even devolution.

Please note that I am not talking about observational science, which is something all cultures have done for thousands of years for survival (but it was not called science).

The mind boggles!

Why go to Mars when we are creating it on Earth? Only an insane, ego-driven obtuse system would ruin its home planet by using up its precious and dwindling resources to make itself rich enough and powerful enough to set up a colony on another planet. Why would we disregard and disrespect where we live, and use up precious resources to set up colonies in places we don't belong? There is not even oxygen on Mars, for Gaia's sake! Wouldn't we just take that same disrespectful consciousness with us and ruin another planet?

Mars is far enough away but still important in its rotational and gravitational relationship to Earth. However, the moon is integral to the balance of our planet. Its presence helps to stabilise our planet's wobble and moderate our climate, and it plays an integral part in the ocean and tides. Knowing this about the moon, what sort of insane people are happy to go there to blast it, mine it, fight to own it and very possibly throw it off its axis? Who knows what lengths these egoic conquerors will go to for wealth? Earth will be so impacted by their actions that I just want to cry about the insanity of the people who rule our capitalist patriarchy and who have no regard for what they do to planet Earth.

Reflections to reflect on

- What makes us different from other animals? Is it not that we are capable of thinking and acting beyond our biology?
- Yet, most of the human race are sleepwalkers, followers and incapable of original thought.
- Is this why we have had and still have such disastrous experiences with dictatorships?
- Is it once again that the majority are sleepwalking while the few who are awake risk their lives for the greater good?
- Having been a worrier and a warrior for the future throughout my life, I ask myself, has it been worth it?

CHAPTER 6

PLASTIC

Plastic is not fantastic; it is drastic and drastically needs to be reduced or it will kill us all. It decorates the sea environment by fragmenting itself into smaller pieces and as it breaks down, it transforms itself to look like its surroundings. Microplastics are in the air we breathe, in the earth's atmosphere and are affecting the climate. It has infiltrated the whole planet and everything that lives here.[20]

Plastic is a chameleon – it is often indistinguishable from the natural environment. It is malleable at birth and in death in the way it breaks down, giving it the versatility to survive. What if that means that eventually, it will be in the cellular structure of everything, including humans? Is it an artificial inanimate intelligence created by us, and have we given it life without thought of its long-term destructive nature? If it does not eventually kill us, will it assimilate as part of our body structure? If so, what sort of humans will we become? How would we be structurally and mentally affected? More pliable, more brittle, more defective?

The incidence of cancer in the last 50 years has increased at an unimaginable rate and is still rising: could it be that as plastic products increase, so does cancer? Of course, there are many factors contributing to the increase of cancer like diet, alcohol, poisons, pesticides, pollution and chemicals to name a few. Could the ingestion of plastic that is now so microscopic the body may find it difficult to expel, therefore weaken and compromise the body as it attempts to deal with the infiltration of a foreign substance but has no defences other than to surround it with extra cells?

The sea absorbs plastic, breaking it up into such little pieces that sea flora bonds around it, incorporating it into its core. Fauna then eats it, causing widespread death. I have coined the word "plastangle weed" to describe the often-indistinguishable mix of plastic entangled in seaweed I find daily on the beach. Today, 200 million metric tons of plastic is currently in the oceans, and 11 million metric tons flow into our oceans every year.[21] It ensnares the marine animals we cherish and the fish we put on our plates. It even appears in the table salt we use and is found in our bodies.

Plastic has become an artificial entity able to infiltrate its environment. Will plastic eventually filter through the layers of the earth and reach its core, where it will burn alongside the organic material and cause even more toxic fumes to circulate in the atmosphere? Will anything that needs to breathe be able to survive?

The world's first synthetic plastic was Bakelite, invented in 1907 by Belgian-American Leo Baekeland. Other scientists jumped on the bandwagon and developed it further until

Herman Staudinger, "the father" of polymer chemistry, topped them all by discovering a polymer that became an important commercial plastic. The man whose research supported the rapid growth of the plastics industry won a Nobel Laureate for his work in 1953. This is just one of many examples where we have blindly allowed science to create disastrous environmental messes and rewarded them for it.

Reflections to reflect on

- Plastic is the silent killer!
- Will plastic in the end be our demise?
- Recycling plastic is still plastic being made.
- Have we become like plastic, mindless and drastic?
- Let's not continue to make "plastangle" weed the new beach flora, killing us through our wildlife.

CHAPTER 7

UNSUSTAINABLE WORLD POPULATION

The eighteenth-century philosopher Thomas Malthus predicted that humanity's insatiable urge to reproduce and overpopulate would have dire consequences. This urge to reproduce would become an overwhelming force pushing the earth's limited resources to the point of making subsistence for all creatures, including humans, difficult to sustain and quite likely taking us prematurely into the 6th mass extinction. He also predicted that with over population, food resources would become scarce and we would die in a mass famine.[22]

In an article in *The Georgia Straight* (2011), David Suzuki reports that he once asked the great ecologist E.O. Wilson how many people the planet could sustain indefinitely? Wilson responded: "If you want to live like North Americans, 200 million. North Americans, Europeans, Japanese and Australians, who make up 20 per cent of the world's population, are consuming more than 80 per cent of the world's resources. We are the major predators and despoilers of the planet. Keep in mind, though, that most environmental devastation is not directly caused by individuals or households, but by corporations driven more by profits than human needs."[23]

Currently, the Western world holds 20 per cent of the world's 8 billion people and it is already using more than its share of the resources. The other 80 per cent – more than 6 billion people, which includes China, India, Africa and most of South America – wants to live the same way as we do in the West. The consequences are not difficult to calculate. We have already passed the level of sustainability regardless of what the scientists say. We have two options: drastically decrease the population or decrease the levels of consumption of the developed Western countries. However, by reducing the population, we will also start to unshackle ourselves from capitalism and decrease consumption of resources at the same time.

Earth's capacity

According to E.O. Wilson in his book *The Future of Life* (2003), "The constraints of the biosphere are fixed."[24]

Does this not call for alarm and action from all of us to stop and find new ways to save the planet and ourselves?

A world that can only just sustain humans surely cannot be a healthy sustainable world. Plants and animals need healthy environments to survive as well – and if they don't survive on the planet, nor will we. Humans need a biodiverse planet to survive but the planet does not need humans to survive. In fact, we are a threat to its survival. The activities of our species are creating global climate change and destroying habitats at an alarming rate.

Destruction of forests

Research data shows that 10,000 years ago, 71 per cent of the land's surface was covered by forests, shrubs and grasslands. Today, almost half of this has been replaced with urban development and agriculture, and most of the destruction has taken place over the last 300 years as the population has increased.[25]

If this is allowed to continue, a child born today will most definitely struggle to survive under the conditions of global deforestation. The destruction of forests leads to a lack of oxygen, an increase in carbon dioxide, decreased purification of the atmosphere and an acceleration of rising temperatures. In addition, deforestation drives the spread of diseases and viruses normally contained by a healthy forest, leading to an increase in infectious disease transmission in humans.[26]

Without forests to absorb and filtrate rainfall, topsoil and nutrients will wash away, resulting in massive soil erosion. There would be no water storage and underground aquifers would not be replenished. Without forests the atmosphere's humidity by transpiration which affects rainfall and climate would be thrown out of balance.

Is this not sounding like the climate change we are starting to experience now?

Without forests the range of ecosystems on earth would simply disappear. Yet knowing this we are cutting down forests at an alarming rate to line the pockets of capitalism.

A tree in the Amazon rainforest is home to thousands of species. I ask what sort of uncaring, unfeeling species have we developed into to be able to justify this kind of genocide of another species? It's not only forest ecosystems being destroyed in the hands of capitalism and over population but also population growth occurring in or close to biodiversity hotspots. Large amounts of flora and fauna are being destroyed in these regions, due to significant migration of people who are facing poverty in these areas and need forest resources for financial gain. This is slowing down urgent conservation efforts, placing the whole planet in peril yet again.

There is so much information available online describing what is happening with deforestation that it is overwhelming. It's happening so fast that it cannot accurately be measured. The environmental impact is so dire, only an obtuse economic system obsessed with making money at any cost would be so careless as not to do something drastic and urgent about it. And only a population of humans so deluded, who do not care enough to inform themselves to stop it happening, would allow this to happen under their watch.

There are so many consequences to deforestation that it brings me tears, despair and disbelief that this is really happening to our beautiful planet.

This is only a handful of the disturbing facts on deforestation – sadly, there are too many to list.
- Raising cattle for beef accounts for 41% of deforestation worldwide while soy and palm oil are significant contributors too. [27] Over two thirds of food products we eat every day contain palm oil. Even chocolate

biscuits – for Gaia's sake, stop buying these products and start cooking! The soap and shampoo you use is also likely made from palm oil and the list goes on.
- We replace these forests with monoculture plantations destroying habitat which is not only endangering but making many species reliant on the forests extinct.
- Soil erosion, flooding and the ability to absorb water which feeds the planets deep water reserves is also lost in deforestation.
- Cutting down trees not only releases stored carbon into the atmosphere but the loss of trees limits the ability to absorb existing carbon dioxide from the atmosphere, which contributes significantly to climate change.
- Deforestation not only contributes to the spreading of diseases but also introduces new diseases into the human population.

Trees are so sacred and essential to survival, that even removing trees from your property or nature strip (especially large established trees) causes not only a major injustice, but also impacts on your immediate environment's ability to contribute to the absorption of carbon dioxide.

Destruction of oceans

The oceans, the earth's main cleansing and rejuvenating systems, are struggling with not only the amount of plastic but all the other toxic substances we irresponsibly pour into them. Sea creatures, which are integral to the health of the oceans, are ingesting these substances and dying at an alarming rate. An international team of ecologists and economists predicted back in 2006 that the world's oceans will be empty of fish by 2048 due to overfishing, pollution, habitat loss and climate change.[28] A four-year study of the ecosystems of 7,800 marine species around the world concluded that same year that the world's stocks of seafood will have collapsed by 2050, based on the rates of destruction by fishing recorded in 2006.[29]

The collapse of ocean biodiversity and the catastrophic collapse of phytoplankton and zooplankton populations in the sea will in turn cause the collapse of civilisation, and most likely the extinction of the human species. Is it possible to organise ourselves as a world population to not eat from the sea or pollute it, in order to restore it to health in the hope of one day being able to sustainably eat fish again?

I often think to myself how deluded people are when they say, "I am a vegetarian who eats fish," as if protesting about the meat industry. A pescatarian is causing even more damage to our ecosystem because when the sea is fished out and dead, so are we.

Food production

While some scientists may claim that 10 billion people is the uppermost population limit where food is concerned, this is only possible if everyone becomes vegetarian. This is extremely unlikely and therefore Wilson's estimation that food resources will fall short of the 10 billion population mark is very likely. The other factors are the nitrogen cycle, the available quantities of phosphorus and atmospheric carbon concentrations on our planet.

How often have I heard people say, "It's not the size of the population, but the distribution of resources alone is the problem." The real problem is delusional capitalism at work and because we are not comfortable dealing with the population issues, we take on that delusion without question.

Left unchecked, climate change aligned with population explosion and low agricultural yields will drastically increase global poverty and hunger over the next two decades, warns the international aid organisation, Oxfam, in a report released in May 2011. In the report, Oxfam predicts the prices of staple foods such as corn and rice will climb by 180 per cent and 130 per cent, respectively, by the year 2030.[30]

Let's face it: human-introduced elements like plastic, global warming, overpopulation, destruction of the ecosystem, and wars have created the precarious world we live in.

World population growth

The following graph[31] charts population growth through the years, showing the length of time it has taken for the population to increase by one billion. In 1803, our population reached its first billion and it took just 124 years to reach our second. From 1975 to 2011 our population increased by 1 billion every 12 years.

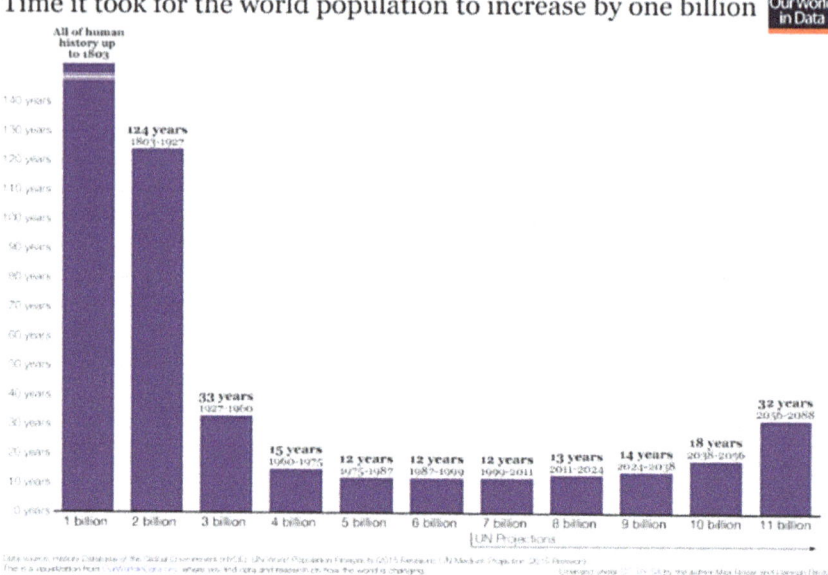

I think we have already reached and surpassed a safe population capacity, and continual growth – even at a slower rate – is not just irresponsible, it is suicidal. If we all want to live as we do in the Western culture, at the rate we are growing and pillaging the planet, as E.O. Wilson suggests, we can only sustain 200 million of us.

Logical illogical consequence

Does science create more problems than solutions? We are already out of control and science has not yet dealt with the existing problems. Continuing to allow the population to increase will end with a situation where there is no way out for us but cannibalism – when we as humans will be the only meat left to eat.

Another issue is we have too many laws and more are developing. In my mind, the more laws we need means we have too many people to bring order. Being like robots makes us easier to control and the more laws, the more restrictions are put on us – making us too afraid to do anything. Revolution will arrive but with so many 'asleep' people, the revolution for sustainability could at best become as large as a minority in any culture.

Controlling us in crowds

The more of us there are, the less likely it is that we can mobilise change. We are so disconnected from each other and our community that we don't care about anything other than ourselves and what we can have, giving as little as possible in return. We humans are easily led and brainwashed into believing whatever the most dominant power wants us to think, and with so many of us taking on different powerful belief systems, we become immobilised. The many different belief systems in our world cause us to become confused; making it impossible to agree on anything is how we are controlled.

Focusing on survival for the individual is the perfect way to control us because we all have different ways of surviving. We cannot form communities because we no longer know how to – we are too busy being individuals and believing that we have a choice. This has led to social fragmentation, where people are cut from the herd. We feel less compassion because we are competing to survive and no longer have the ability to work or think cooperatively or communally.

Compliance is complicit!

We are constant polluters – we cannot help ourselves. We even think we have the right to do so. We cannot have everyone live as we do, and we have no right to live this way. Living in small, self-sufficient, sustainable communities is how we stop polluting on such a grand scale. We are not watching where we step: we are so self-obsessed that we trample on nature without a second thought about what is beneath our feet. We must leave as small a footprint as possible – cities are paved to keep nature away and the concrete makes us lose this awareness.

I ask myself what would I do if my child was unwell? Would I not care for her, nurture her until her health was restored? Yet it seems that we see ourselves as separate from the earth so continue to pollute the oceans and eat and misuse everything that lives in it at a ferocious rate. At this point of our civilisation, we must care for the earth like it is our sick child to bring her back to health. For everyone's sake.

We lost our way and connection to the earth's vibrational energy when we started wearing shoes. Before shoes we "watched our step", we were careful and respectful with every step and we walked by treading lightly on the earth. When walking barefooted our head is naturally slightly tilted towards the ground changing our stance to a humble one.

If not careful with stepping, bare feet could easily be injured. Wearing shoes has made us careless, arrogant and has disconnected us from the vibrational energy of the earth and also deprived us of foot stimulation which helps other parts of the body vibrationally and energetically.

Shoes have also disconnected us from the awareness that every bit of ground we step on is home to some creature, often microscopic. Treading lightly on the earth, causing little disturbance, is respectful. I dare you to take your shoes off and start walking barefooted as often as possible and see how much respect you have for where and how you walk. If we must wear shoes, choose soft, flexible and thin-soled shoes. When the vibration of your tread does not stop the frogs from croaking then you know that you are treading lightly.

> **QUESTIONS TO PONDER**
>
> - Have we become so arrogant that we believe being at the top of the food chain comes with no responsibility to look after the planet?
> - Is the ability to make conscious choices not what sets us apart from other animals? (At least they are smart enough not to destroy what enables them the privilege of life.)
> - Is it possible to stop eating from the sea and polluting for at least 10 years to give it a long enough rest, so we may one day be able to sustainably eat fish again?
> - Are there just too many of us to agree on anything?
> - Are there too many of us to organise anything on a mass scale? It appears that the more of us there are, the less we can think and act collectively and communally.
> - What of the perception that science will save us from ourselves?
> - Or is it that we need to save ourselves from science?
> - Do scientists really know what they are doing?
> - Do we blindly place too much trust in science?

Population solution

A simple snip and *voila*, a vasectomy. This one action for every man, except those who are accredited for fathering, will release us all from the clutches of patriarchy and capitalism. Not only will it free women from the constant mother role but men will also be freed from the constant provider role. The very unhealthy nuclear family structure will start to break down and we will be free to explore more diverse ways of relating to each other.

My observations with the nuclear family structure are that it appears perfect on the outside but is fraught with difficulties on the inside, leading to tolerated unhappiness and abuse for the sake of security and fitting in. The other advantage for vasectomising most men is that we can start to control the precariously large numbers of humans we have created under the false belief that our home, Gaia, is endlessly abundant. If we don't start organising ourselves to become a sustainable population of 2 billion worldwide, it's been nice knowing you!

I can hear ignorant and arrogant voices sounding outraged as they say, "No-one can tell me if I can or can't have children" and "I have rights you know – how dare you!" People can scream and shout about their right to freedom of choice all they like but if they think freedom is about having a choice, they should think again. Unfortunately, their screaming will eventually lead us into oblivion.

We need to regroup ASAP and organise ourselves to reduce the population drastically. And don't think that we in Australia aren't to blame for the size of the population. We darling Australians, along with the rest of the First World, may produce only 20 per cent of the population but I'm ashamed to say that we consume 80 per cent of the earth's resources. Our lifestyle is coveted by many from around the world but without the awareness that living in abundance will not sustain any of us for very long.

The words "science and technology will save us" are such a cop out! Are we so blind that we cannot see how technology and capitalism are the major destroyers of our ability to provide for ourselves? That we have become reliant on the power of technology and what it feeds us with? We are also blindly accepting of ego-based science, pretty much giving it carte blanche to create abominations just because it can, allowing it to destroy and disrupt the natural order and the fabric of our home, Gaia, for our pleasure and to our detriment. Living in a so-called democracy does not give us the right to destroy our planet.

CALCULATION TO REACH POPULATION TARGET

In 2023 we will have approximately 8 billion people; we need to reduce that to 2 billion for long-term sustainability. Twenty years of no births equals a reduction of 120 million, bringing the total down to 6.8 billion. After 20 years, we would still have many people left of breeding age. At the 20-year mark, we reproduce at 5 million births per year worldwide. Sixty million deaths occur worldwide each year. Take 5 million births from that per year to get 55 million deaths per year. Multiply 55 million by 90 years to get 4.95 billion. Take that from 6.8 billion and this gives us 1.8 billion. This brings us close to our target within 110 years.

Note: the above calculation is approximate and is on a straight-line basis, not on a compounding basis. It is included for illustrative purposes only.

While 110 years sounds like a long time, considering one human can live for 100 years, it's realistic. One of the advantages of taking that amount of time is that it allows us to adjust incrementally into new and more sustainable communities.

As humans, we can and do accomplish such amazing feats that it is hard to believe we can't organise ourselves out of extinction. My rudimentary calculation is based on bringing the population down to a sustainable number, which is approximately 2 billion, as quickly as possible. As the population becomes smaller and as we adapt to a new paradigm, we will be able to start forming smaller, more sustainable communities where the number of children born will be limited and cared for by that community.

This is a start in taking responsibility for the future of the human species.

Ideas for population reduction

As mentioned before, vasectomies are an easy and safe process and a proactive solution to reducing our populations at a reasonable speed. The beauty of vasectomies is they are reversible, and the male gene pool can be changed to avoid inbreeding. Women, who are the birth givers, can also be changed to avoid inbreeding. Regularly changing the breeders reduces the risk of inbreeding and gives a variety of breeders the opportunity to do so. The children born will be shared and cared for by a community – the old saying "It takes a community to raise a child," will apply.

To achieve this restructure, we would need to set up small communities which share space and interweave with other communities. I believe that as our population reduces, this will become easier and as we learn and teach our children to live in communities, we will learn to get along with each other and care for each other like the ancient civilisations did.

There is no doubt in my mind that at the rate we are destroying the planet and at our pleasure, our unhealthy and unbalanced planet will continuously try to adjust to find balance for itself. In the process, we will deal with a great loss of human life and human habitat through pandemics and environmental catastrophes. In the year 2022, we are already experiencing an increase in environmental disasters, and it will get worse until we start to control our out-of-control population and behaviour.

Humans are mammals gone viral

This will upset many people, especially those who are arrogantly ignorant enough to have no humility and who are oblivious to the damage we, as one of the species inhabiting the earth, are causing. We are the most unconscious of all the species when it comes to adapting sustainably to our environment.

How often have I heard a human say that animals or birds are stupid, because they continue to nest where they walk with their dogs or near their lawn (which is mowed in its nesting area). We are so self-important and I might add clueless enough that preservation and coexistence with another creature escapes us.

As our population decreases, systems will change and with that, new opportunities to create a new more sustainable existence will commence. Even if what I am saying sounds ludicrous, we will find down the track we will have to come to grips with it. Just like wearing masks, and having our movements restricted and every move monitored were scoffed at before the 2020 pandemic.

Imagine the freedom of a culture where men are vasectomised and both women and men are not bound by their biology. Isn't that what sets us apart from other animals – the ability to think and act beyond our biology? In my observation women who consciously practise celibacy – not from religious dogma, but as a way to reach self-empowerment – say that it can be an immensely powerful tool for reaching personal power. While consciously celibate, one is not bound or controlled by the folly of the treadmill most of us live on. I am not suggesting that this is the only way or necessarily a lifelong practice, but I can say that if practised for a reasonable amount of time, it changes our expectations of others and life. Relationships take on a new meaning, where once they were needs-based and mistaken for love (one of the most misused and misunderstood words). Relationships gain an equality of flow where friendship and companionship prevail, replacing relationships bound by neediness and expectation, and defined by the physical act of sex.

Practising celibacy is very freeing from emotional ties, clears the head and allows more time for enjoyable, creative pursuits that are not sexually based. Maybe if we did this for a while, we would discover new ways of relating and our emotional needs would lessen, allowing truer relationships based on love and not emotional attachment.

So how we will decide who is to have children? To begin with, it will seem harsh, and it may have to be done by some government structure but hopefully we will be evolved enough not to find ourselves in a situation like *The Handmaid's Tale* (Atwood, 1985). Once we start the process, we may also find that as time goes by, both women and men are released from the present paradigm of the nuclear family and having children – its *raison d'etre* – for the benefit of both the patriarchal and capitalist systems. Once men and especially women are liberated from thinking that having children is their major purpose in life, newfound freedom occurs, and a new world order will begin to appear. This will give us more time and energy to dedicate to working towards creating balance for the human species, which is in harmony with the planet. After all, good planets are hard to find!

Understanding everything I say and suggest in this book is going to require humans with a highly evolved consciousness and awareness who can unite for the greater good. This is highly improbable since most humans are overgrown babies with their hands in Mother Nature's till. Of course, my suggestions are highly unlikely to be implemented – but they are not impossible and offer a way through this mess.

Reflections to reflect on

- They sell us all the products that make us think we can become and achieve what we covet – only we covet what's fed to us and we will never know what or who we truly are unless we get off the treadmill and stay off it.
- We then move to "inaction" and hope. Hope is a deep-rooted survival mechanism, and we usually resort to hope when there is none. Yet hope followed by action is hope "in action" and a different thing.
- Information Age or Disinformation Age?
- Poverty isn't just about money.
- We must care for the earth like it is our sick child or our sick mother to bring her back to health because our children will become motherless without a planet.

CHAPTER 8

WATER

Water is essential for life and it must be respected, used wisely and harvested without environmental damage. As population growth increases and the planet becomes hotter and dryer, there will be increased demand on this precious resource and future wars will likely be about the ownership of water.

Although 70 per cent of the earth is water, its distribution is extremely uneven – 96.5 per cent is salt water found in oceans, with fresh water making up just 3.5 per cent. Of this limited amount of fresh water, the vast majority is not accessible to us – more than 68 per cent is frozen in ice and glaciers, and another 30 per cent is located below the ground![32]

With a current population of nearly 8 billion people, and only a tiny percentage available for human use, fresh water is clearly a finite resource. Overpopulation and an aggressive capitalist system is rapidly disrupting the finely tuned equilibrium of the freshwater cycle, which has sustained life on our planet for many thousands of years.

Some of the man-made disturbances that threaten the planet's finely tuned equilibrium are:

- Overpopulation and increasing demand on water
- Desalination plants
- Global warming increasing water vapour in the atmosphere
- Inappropriate use of water table reserves.

Desalination

Over the last 50 years, the number of desalination plants has steadily increased, so that today, there are over 20,000 installed across the world.[33] Desalination plants are an act of desperation rather than a solution born from wisdom. Not only do they cause irreversible environmental damage, but the operation costs are substantial too.

As water becomes scarcer, desalination is (unfortunately for us and the environment) becoming a leading growth area. Instead of looking for long-term sustainable solutions, private global corporations are turning desalination water into a commodity and are setting themselves up to sell water for a profit. This will make it more difficult to control and ensure public safety.

I ask what sort of country has a government who not only sells their precious water resource to private companies but also allows desalination to happen and leaves it in the control of a money-making companies? Is this not the work of a government controlled by capitalism?

As usual, in the patriarchal capitalist system, we find short-sighted, so-called solutions for problems we have created which are not sustainable, instead of addressing the real issues such as overpopulation, climate change and deforestation among many others. We simply go ahead and create more havoc in the name of the survival of the human species, not realising or refusing to realise that we are not important to the survival of a healthy, vibrant planet. Yet the other species on the planet are. Without them, there would be no ecosystem, nor the biodiversity needed to sustain a healthy planet on which human life can exist.

Water vapour

Water vapour is one of the largest contributors to the earth's greenhouse effect — although it does not control the earth's temperature, it is controlled by the temperature.

According to American scientist Andrew Dessler, data shows that as surface temperature increases, so too does atmospheric humidity. "Dumping greenhouse gases into the atmosphere makes the atmosphere more humid and since water vapour is itself a greenhouse gas, the increase in humidity amplifies the warming from carbon dioxide."[34]

Digging deeper and using reserves

The Great Artesian Basin (GAB) covers 22 per cent of Australia's land base and it is one of the largest underground freshwater systems in the world. The GAB flows underground through parts of Queensland, New South Wales, South Australia and the Northern Territory. However, it is not an endless supply of fresh water. Unregulated bore drilling was allowed to happen for more than 150 years, resulting in significant wastage and environmental damage of this precious resource. As a species, we have this insane notion that resources are endless and at our disposal!

In the 1980s, bore capping commenced in Queensland to rehabilitate the GAB, and since then naturally occurring artesian springs have emerged in places they had not previously been seen.[35] This demonstrates the ability of the natural world to repair itself when we stop interfering and give it a chance.

Water as a commodity

We are already a dry country – only an insane political culture would allow a resource as precious as water to be sold to foreign investors like it has been in Australia. Water should not be treated as a commodity; it is a life-sustaining element that needs to be respected and cared for like our lives depend on it, because they do. Without fresh, clean water there is no life. According to the Federal Government's Register of Foreign Ownership of Water Entitlements, released in March 2019, 10.4 per cent of Australia's water entitlements have a level of foreign ownership. [36]

It is interesting to note that indigenous Australians and indeed all First Nations peoples across the world have a spiritual connection to all water resources as it is an essential part of their connection to the land and their long-term survival. Unlike us, they see themselves as not being separate from the land and therefore hold great respect for this essential life-giving resource.[37]

However, our culture sees a resource as separate to ourselves and to be used solely for our benefit, disregarding any consequence our actions towards this resource may have on other species who we share the planet with. We just see the planet's resources as something to be used and abused.

Sunscreen and the oceans
Two alarming facts about sunscreen:
- It is estimated that 20,000 tonnes washes off tourists bodies every year in the Mediterranean alone
- Science researchers believe up to 14,000 tonnes are released in coral reef areas every year, causing extensive damage to these precious ecosystems.[38]

As individuals, and as a community, we have blindly accepted that wearing sunscreen and other nasty lotions on our skin will protect us from the sun without having serious consequences on other parts of our environment. While sunscreen may protect us from the dangers of the sun, it is having a disastrous impact on ocean life.

For Gaia's sake! We must do our research before using these products that pollute our oceans and waterways in a major way. If we care about minimising the harm, we need to wear appropriate clothing. Loose cotton light coloured clothing a scarf and a hat are something we have control over and wearing them is not that difficult to do!

> **QUESTIONS TO PONDER**
>
> - How do we prioritise water consumption in the light of global warming and the greater demand this will have on the planet's water supply?
> - Should water be an ownable commodity?
> - What is the future impact on our water supply, considering that at present, 10 per cent of our water in Australia has been sold to major corporations?
> - Will these corporations prioritise the use of water? For example, will they mine first then supply their needs before our needs – especially if ownership is by foreign investors?

Traveller versus tourist

Tourism is another environmental nightmare. They tell us it keeps an economy going – but at what cultural and environmental cost?

A traveller is a person who goes to a place to spend a reasonable amount of time with the locals and their culture, joining them in eating their cultural food, learning about their tradition, and blending into their culture. The traveller doesn't interfere with that culture, and most importantly, the traveller does not impose hers or his own culture on the people of that country. A tourist on the other hand, rushes into a country, tramples all over its cultural and tourist sights, and does it en masse. The tourist then takes endless photos and selfies to show their friends and family that they've been somewhere on their holiday. All without a thought about the cultural and environmental impact their indulgence is contributing. In addition, travellers contribute their money to the local economy whereas tourists' money goes mostly back to the first world.

Tourism creates endless amounts of pollution from the fuel it takes to get there and back, and the amount of plastic it takes to feed and accommodate a tourist, let alone millions of them. There is also the amount of plastic used for the gifts a tourist must buy to take home. Tourism also adds pressure to a country's systems and resources and causes it to change its cultural food and traditions to accommodate tourists' tastes.

Tourism isn't travel; tourism is a destructive virus in pandemic proportions unleashed on the world, consuming ferociously without a reflective thought on its impact on the long-term survival of the planet and ourselves. We can no longer environmentally afford this luxury. Even travel these days is time and population size prohibitive. What a dilemma!

What is this insatiable need for tourism especially since we are now aware of the environmental cost of such indulgences? Is it to escape from our lives even for just a short moment? Is it to keep up with the Joneses so that we can show the world on social media how amazing we are to have been somewhere and contributed further to our ignorance of the damage we are causing? Or, worst of all, creating tourism as something to covet?

Is it once again pressure from our capitalist economy to create an insatiable want in us to make us feel that unless we are tourists, we will never be happy?

What can we put in place in our lives and in our own or nearby environment to take us to a place of escape and rejuvenation? After all travel and tourism can be stressful and very tiring.

Since it seems that governments don't have the courage to impose a yearly carbon use allocation per person – is it not our responsibility to do it for ourselves and start prioritising our own carbon allocation?

> **Reflections to reflect on**
>
> - It is time to take responsibility and start a self-imposed carbon allocation scheme.
> - Travel when absolutely necessary.
> - Tourism is no longer a mindless joy-ride but a serious indulgence the planet cannot afford.
> - Be creative and responsible with your need to escape.
> - No matter how far you go there is no escape only delusion.

Part 2

Connecting and relating

CHAPTER 9

MOTHERHOOD

Motherhood is a virtue – or is it?
While women in all cultures expect to have children, within patriarchy, motherhood is bestowed as the ultimate experience for a woman – the only other roles being the maid and the "sexual object". Although I'm sure motherhood has its advantages in our culture, unfortunately it is something that is assumed for women regardless of whether they want children or not, hence the patriarchal saying to keep a woman "barefoot and pregnant". Even though we believe this is normal, women living and raising children in the nuclear family is far from normal and on many levels, is the most unnatural and often destructive way to bring up children and to live in general.

Danger of the nuclear family
Having children in the nuclear family structure is its *raison d'être*. We see what happens when a couple can't have children: they will go to extreme lengths such as IVF and surrogacy to have them, even though we live in a world that is perilously overpopulated. If there are no children,

what is the point of the nuclear family? Heaven help us if women and men have enough in common to make a life worth living without children.

Before the nuclear family, people lived and worked together in a biological community. This is the healthiest and most natural way to live, not only for children but for the sustainable biodiversity of the planet and the longevity of the human race. The nuclear family was developed first with the onset of patriarchy and then for the convenience of industrialisation – nuclear families were more flexible and mobile so they could move from pastoral areas to the cities where the work was, for the accumulation of wealth of the few. The nuclear family also serves capitalism due to each household needing to own products, which in a community style of living could be shared.

I wonder whether the nuclear family model of children being raised by the woman in a house on her own with some or little help from the husband, rather than in a community of people, is isolating and therefore creates an unhealthy dependency of women on their children? When women are unhappy, consciously or unconsciously, does this family structure become a "time bomb" waiting to explode?

Also, what is the impact on children reared in the nuclear family? I guess we don't need to look too far for that answer. Among many of the problems our children are facing, statistics on the increase in child suicide are readily available. Mothers seem to live in an emotional prison of perpetual guilt. They also seem to live vicariously through their children, being at their children's mercy and not wanting to be judged by them, or others, as being a bad mother. Yet they feel judged by them all of their lives. A mother is never freed from them and if there is a glimmer of freedom, the grandchildren appear. Hoorah! Once again, she has a role to play and a second chance to be needed.

The structure of the nuclear family makes a woman's status and value in society conditional on being a good mother. Women become consumed and distracted by child-rearing and when there are opportunities to take on major leadership roles, they are restricted by their own and others' expectations that their children come first and at the cost of necessary change in our society. This enables men to become the decision-makers in the political process and leaves women with a very narrow focus in their lives. Given this narrow focus, it is not surprising that women, in general, become obsessive about their children, overprotective and find it difficult to let go.

In this patriarchal culture where children are emotionally owned by their mothers, they are an object to trot out to show how clever and remarkable they are for having produced these extensions of themselves. And if their children don't turn out as expected, the time spent worrying and in guilt tears women away from experiencing their inner personal power and sanctum and playing a critical role in the future of the world.

Capitalism is playing an increasing role in this patriarchal expectation through IVF and surrogacy. For example, in Australia during the 2020 pandemic, a government decision to cope with the increased pressure in hospitals from COVID-19 put a limit on elective surgery, one being IVF. The uproar from this decision reversed IVF from being considered elective surgery. This indicates that the obsession with having children is so out of balance that it is considered more important than painful hip replacements and eye surgery among other medical conditions.

The difference between women and men in wanting to have children is that for women, it gives value and status while for men, it is a symbol of their masculinity and the prowess of their seed.

We may well ask:
Who is the woman without children?
Who is the woman not bred in the patriarchy?
Who is the woman outside the nuclear family?
I am overwhelmed by the amount of oppression I see most women around me in, only nobody notices because it's normal – who is truly the woman outside the confines of marriage?
Who is the man for that matter outside patriarchy and the nuclear family?
Would "new-foggy-family" be a more appropriate name for "new-clear-family?"

Unlike women who have children, I often notice that women who consciously have not had children have a sense of freedom, are not bound by guilt, are not at their children's mercy and disposal, are not waiting to hear from them, and their sense of self-worth isn't dependent on their children. They have more time to contribute to the community, more time for their friends and they are more likely to create a community of friendships while being independent of them at the same time.

In the West, with the aid of capitalism, our obsession with children has led to wanting to give our children everything they want, depriving them of a sense of achievement gained by working for what they want. We have created a culture of instant gratification with an attitude of arrogance and expectation without the consciousness of having to take responsibility for their actions or wants. When we are given everything we want, what else is there to have except for constant dissatisfaction leading to ego malfunction, creating depression and a sense of worthlessness? The "me, me, me" culture becomes dominant and capitalism has won yet again!

I would like to add this comment about the contraceptive pill, which has no name other than its generic one, "the pill", because no-one wants to name it … why not? Not taking the pill will give women's bodies a rest from being bombarded with possible carcinogenic drugs, and the environment would get a rest from the toxic urine women produce when they are on the pill.

Stepping off the treadmill

The treadmill is where one does what everyone else does over and over without question. To jump off the treadmill and create change takes a combination of imagination, intellect, reflective thought and creativity. There are treadmills within treadmills and jumping off the main one is a start. When one can step on and off the treadmill with awareness then one is well on the way to achieving self-empowerment.

Once off the treadmill, there is an adjustment period which can feel a little uncomfortable so jumping straight back on it may feel easier. However, that doesn't give us time to discover wonderful new possibilities. We're so inside our egoic heads and distracted by its voice that we don't know where we are going. The only thing keeping us from bumping into each other is the treadmill and when we get in each other's way, our egoic voices get louder and we think that we, in the Western world, have the right to anything we want without consequences.

By making and falsely giving us a self-righteous belief system, we are kept distracted and perpetually on the treadmill like trained Pavlov's dogs. Our senses are so dulled with science, technology and alcohol that if we get off the treadmill, we feel like hell – not realising that hell is already where we are. When we realise that we are on the treadmill, we fear getting off because not only does it mean stepping into the unknown but we do it on our own. This is especially the case for women who often feel vulnerable without a man.

Regardless of class, many women live in oppressive relationships with an undefinable threat, and they do their best to make it work, often by compromising, rather than face the fear and disruption of ending up on their own. Since one in three women are abused in their lifetime[39] it is very understandable in this culture why women stay on the treadmill. Unknowingly women are the guardians of the treadmill: "The best man for the job is a woman." Women civilise men. In fact, there would be no civilisation without women because men, in general, left on their own would create chaos – possibly even brutality – and become uncivilised.

Of course, the other end of the equation of women being oppressed is women wanting some power balance in our system. Women can become needy and controlling, hence the saying "hen-pecked". I must admit I do see this dynamic often in the nuclear family situation – men can look like victims and feel downtrodden by women. However, this is the result of living in an unnatural social system where there is an imbalance of power.

How liberating it would be for our species to become psychologically healthy, respectful and environmentally aware if given the opportunity to experience a new paradigm of respectful personal power. When we stand in our personal power, we are free to create our own destiny. Stepping off the treadmill brings up fear of being on one's own and feeling vulnerable. Being in power is quite different from having personal power and to achieve personal power for both women and men, one must get off the treadmill and be able to move on and off it as needed or desired.

With personal power, we do not need to oppress or lord over anything or anyone because we are completely self-aware and in tune with our senses. Personal power is what gives us the strength not to be distracted by shiny objects offered to us by capitalism. Self-awareness means using reflection, thoughtfulness, intellect, imagination, creativity and respect – qualities needed for a utopian existence.

QUESTIONS TO PONDER

- Are we not intrinsically tribal?
- Do we not unconsciously yearn for our tribal past?
- Have we lost the ability to think collectively and act communally?
- Is it time to dig into both our human roots and our deep unconscious and ask ourselves how our emotional needs can be better met?
- What do we need to put in place for this to happen?
- Are we so comatose that we can no longer think for ourselves, the future of the planet and the human race?
- Will horror for us be what motivates us into action?
- When will we stop sleepwalking and truly wake up?

Value of community living

A good community is a safe and happy place, where everyone's contribution is appreciated and valued. It is free from poverty and crime because everyone's needs rather than wants are being met. It is a place where participating and learning from each other happens, and there is respect and transgenerational sharing of knowledge.

A good community is also a place where a group of people have a deep connection to each other, share common interests, similar values, feel a sense of belonging and come together to create a living situation that promotes the wellbeing not only of their human community but also the environmental flora and fauna community, integral to the health of the planet.

In a community-based culture, the responsibility of rearing children is shared: no one person is solely responsible, thus freeing women and keeping children safer. Children have the support of the whole community, which looks out for them. In a community, children are better adjusted to life because they grow up in an atmosphere of sharing and learning to be responsible and self-reliant at the same time. In a community environment, child-rearing does not happen behind closed doors like it does in our patriarchal model, in which abuse is quite common. In a community-based culture, women are not isolated, and men have more connection as generic fathers and uncles who play an important role in children's lives.

Is it too late?

We in the West believe the nuclear family is at the height of civilisation and that community living is primal, barbaric and associated with poverty. Therefore, we fear that living in a community would be a loss of our privileges. And that is what the wealth-makers want us to believe.

To create industry for the supply of goods for the Western lifestyle, the wealth-makers have created a slave class of people who are so poor, they will work for pennies. Their communities are no longer able to sustain themselves due to the wealth-makers having carved up and destroyed their natural environment.

The disempowerment of having one's natural environment destroyed creates the illusion that the Western lifestyle is the goal, placing increased demand on our once seemingly vast and now fast-depleting natural resources. This is why, as previously stated, the West has 20 per cent of the world's population and uses 80 per cent of the earth's resources to survive. We do more than survive – we waste!

I am saying that with the knowledge we have now, it is time to look at a new paradigm, one which includes drawing knowledge from the community lifestyle that preceded the nuclear family for the long-term survival of all who call Earth home.

Impact of the nuclear family on children

The nuclear family and the institution of marriage appear solid on the outside but when we scratch the surface, it is a very precarious and mostly dysfunctional way to bring up children. Nuclear families are, in general, emotionally lacking yet we remain caught up in this paradigm. Demonstrated failure of the nuclear family is seen in the rise of single-parent families.

CHILD ABUSE FACTS AND STATISTICS

- Children make up more than a quarter (28%) of all detected trafficking victims.
- Nearly 50 million children across the globe have migrated across or within borders or been forcibly displaced. More than half that number – 28 million – are children who have fled violence and insecurity.
- One-quarter of adults report having been physically abused as children.
- International studies suggest 1 in 5 women and 1 in 13 men report having been sexually abused as a child.
- Every year, an estimated 41,000 children under 15 years of age die from homicide. This number may not represent the whole problem, as a large proportion of deaths due to child abuse are incorrectly attributed to falls, burns, drowning and other causes.[40]

Reflections to reflect on

- Is marriage an arrangement made in jail or even a contract made in jail? Is sexual oppression/expression rampant in the guise of liberation in our present culture?
- Patriarchal men prefer to partner with women who are shorter so that they are looked up to. Do women have to keep shrinking to survive in the patriarchy? Are the images portrayed in the media of women and the difference in size between women and men, increasing? Could this be a subliminal ploy to shrink women into oblivion?
- Over centuries, women's status in the patriarchy has created competition to capture the best provider. The media has played this up in such a way that women are rewarded for their bitchiness. As a result, our daughters believe it's the appropriate way to behave.
- Men have lost chivalry and women think that equality is about rejecting kindness and respect from men. There is also the issue of romantic love, which has been created as a way of keeping women servile and willing to even stay in situations of domestic violence.
- Prey and predators – when women look like prey they will be preyed upon. She is a maid before she marries then she loses her maiden name and becomes a wife, a maid by another name.

CHAPTER 10

FRIENDS, ACQUAINTANCES AND COMPANIONSHIPS

Friends, acquaintances and companionships have the potential to interchange. Outside the nuclear family and our biological relationships, there are other important connections we describe as friends and acquaintances. Neither the word "friend" nor the word "acquaintance" adequately describes what we really experience with these relationships and the fluidity between them. A new word is needed because both have the potential to become the other.

We are all in acquaintanceships in motion, rather than in friendships, which implies belonging to someone. For example, we tend to introduce a friend as "This is my friend, ... ", whereas we start as acquaintances – a contact who we may run into or occasionally invite to an event. We have the potential to become friends just as a friend has the potential to slip back to being an acquaintance. What if we had a new word to describe this play between friend and acquaintance? Would this new word create a deeper understanding of our relationship? A new word that comes to mind is "amiquaintance". Apart from our very deep emotionally intimate relationships, at any given time the rest of our connections could be better described as "amiquaintances".

Companionship

What is the difference between companionship and friendship?

Does companionship describe our intimate relationships better than words like husband and wife? As we all know, words like husband, wife, partner, de facto or friendship describe ownership of someone or belonging to someone. Yet these relationships are also fluid like reality.

There is also a non-binding commitment to the essence of the word "companionship" because it more accurately describes a relationship made of mutual love rather than one of lust and dependency mistaken for love. Once again, our patriarchal cultural structure of relationships continues to dominate the way we relate to each other. Unless we have a level of self-awareness, the relationships we believe are the norm will continue to be ones of ownership, in which true self-expression is impeded.

I'm also pondering the concept of marriage and wonder if any one person can fill the position of being everything to another person physically and emotionally? I wonder if it's simpler to treat everyone in our life as our companion without formalisation? This way it's driven by meaningful exchanges rather than expectation? It may be a bit idealistic but if we all shifted our ideas on relationships and strived to reach personal power instead, it would be a much freer way of relating. People may not need so many pets to fulfil the inadequacies of present notions of relationships, especially the nuclear family model.

A healthy way of relating would be to focus on being in a healthy relationship with oneself. This must be our life work if we want to engage in truly positive relationships based on mutual respect. When we move towards self-acceptance, self-love and understanding, we start to value ourselves and when we feel contentment being on our own, we can walk beside others with no need for ownership and exclusivity. To achieve this relationship with ourselves, I recommend celibacy for at least five years for both men and women (with no taboo on self-pleasuring) and if we can live alone, all the better.

Once we achieve self-empowerment then all our relationships have the potential to be free-flowing and fall in with the word "amiquaintance" rather than any of the other words that describe our relationships. Words are important and language defines our reality. In terms of our relationship, the words we use now define the limitations of what our relationships can be. While we use limiting ownership words, we will continue to have confined, limited relationships.

Because we limit the nature of our relationships, we limit their quality and their ability to satisfy us or meet our expectations: perhaps this is the reason we turn to pets?

THE WEBS WE WEAVE

The webs we weave like safety nets that act like traps around our lives.

Inside the webs made of silver threads we bounce around with all our friends.

We fear to fall through the holes between the silver threads and so we weave and weave our illusionary webs all around ourselves and everybody else until the light cannot get in and we don't see a thing.

We forget that the eternal silver thread will infinitely stretch and stretch to keep us safe on the path to meet ourselves and when we meet ourselves, we find ourselves to be nothing more than the silver thread itself.

Reflections to reflect on

- Our intelligence and ability to think is what makes us creative, however most of us are still operating unconsciously with the instincts of animal consciousness and animal impulses but with the aid of the very destructive weapons we have mindlessly created for the purpose of control and power.
- Once we achieve self-empowerment then all our relationships become amiquaintances.
- The expectation that one person can fulfil all your needs for a lifetime is a "fool-filled" expectation.
- The Cinderella complex is a patriarchal concept imposed on girls to make them believe that they will be looked after by a man when they grow up, impairing them to learn the skills of independence.
- Unshackle yourself from needy sexual attachment and celebrate celibacy instead.

CHAPTER 11

PET OBSESSION

There are over 29 million pets in Australia today – more than the estimated human population of 25 million. Over 60 per cent of Australian households own a pet today, and of these, 40 per cent are dogs and 27 per cent are cats. The pet industry is worth billions, with Australians spending over $13 billion on pet services and products in 2019 alone.[41]

In our culture, it seems pets are our substitute when our fellow humans aren't fulfilling us, our emotional needs aren't being met and we are not able to meet them ourselves. Unsatisfactory relationships leave us needy – to want and keep wanting. We need pets, we need children, we need stuff. Capitalist humanity is on a trajectory of endless need; with capitalism and social media we lose emotional and spiritual intelligence, and we become disconnected from ourselves and each other.

Pets and the environment

We are social creatures and need human interaction but our culture by its structure divorces us from emotional self-fulfilment and feeling fulfilled by others of our species.

Due to this, we develop needy requirements for closeness and what is the next best thing? A pet!

Unfortunately for the planet and ourselves, having a pet becomes the norm and we mindlessly think that this is a solution to our dysfunction as humans. I live in a rural town near some spectacular coastline which supports many sand dunes once used by the indigenous people of Australia for shelter and food. The area around this coastline holds great significance for them and, for those who can feel energetic presence, it is very powerful. Before I moved here, I had regularly visited this area for more than 35 years. However, in the last four years, the area has been discovered by many people and their pets. As more people come here, more of the natural environment is destroyed due to dogs and cats running around causing destruction. Worst of all, most people are oblivious to it! Why do people come to these beautiful and spectacular natural areas then start to destroy the very thing that drew them here in the first place? They build large, unnecessary houses and allow their dogs to chase and terrorise the animals that live in the coastal bushland. They also allow their dogs to run over the beach nests of birds who have nested here for thousands of years. And when asked to keep their dogs on the lead and off the soft sand, they become outraged and aggressive as if it is their God-given right to do whatever they want.

For most people, their dogs rule them. Their dogs and their rights have become more important than the survival of the planet and the creatures that inhabit it. Humans are so selfish and unconscious that we – with our dogs, cats and children – believe our right to destroy the planet is more important than its survival.

What delusion are we humans in?

When made aware of our impact, we say things like: "Well these birds are stupid – why are they nesting where we walk – why have they not adapted?" I ask myself: *Who is stupid? And who is it that hasn't adapted to their environment?* I am sure it's not the birds or the animals.

I have run into humans who take great pride in telling me they let their dog loose in the coastal bush to chase anything it wants every day. I am not surprised that our native animals, who live in a diminishing habitat, are dying to the point of extinction.

Let me put it into perspective: if I lived on a quarter-acre block and that was the only habitat I had left to live in, and it was diminishing, and on this block I grew my food and procreated, with the everyday threat of many wild, large uncontrollable wolves which had been let loose in my space to trample all over my food, terrorise me and my children, and even eat my babies, I would be a very stressed, unhappy person. I would be living in constant fear with the prospect of a shortened life span and possible extinction.

As I say, why go to Mars when we are creating it on Earth? As far as I'm concerned, why don't we all go to Mars and give this planet a rest? We have become mindless morons!

In my observation, we mindless morons may also be kind and caring people who think we are doing the right thing for ourselves and others, but that kindness is misguided and it must be redirected into kindness for the ground we walk on, planet Earth and all that call her home. It seems that when humans move to a beach, they see it as mandatory to have dogs as companions – like an accessory trend. Unfortunately for the environment, dogs need exercise and to exercise them we so love to throw a stick or a ball for them, mindlessly allowing them to trample all over ancient sensitive areas with the arrogance that it is our human right because we love our dogs. And often one dog is not enough: "My dog needs a companion otherwise it might get lonely." Is that a projection, or what? Wake up, people!

How many times have we heard, "My dog is well-behaved, it does not chase birds," or "No, my cat doesn't kill anything." Well, someone's cat and dog must be doing it because pet cats kill 83 million native reptiles and 80 million native birds in Australia each year.[42] In 2011, a study in Tasmania found that dogs may be a more serious problem than cats for native wildlife – data showed that after motor vehicles, pet dogs were the next highest cause of wildlife injuries and deaths.[43]

My local shire council does nothing about it, yet at the start of each decision-making meeting, its members acknowledge the ancestral custodians of this land as if to absolve themselves from the disccissions they are about to make aiding in the destruction of the environment that the ancestral custodians cared for, for thousands of years. This is the ultimate hypocrisy! This is the hypocrisy practised by this entire nation called Australia. Shame on us!

Impact of pets

Owning a pet adds unnecessary pressure to our diminishing natural environment. It is not only that pet waste left on the ground causes contamination but also pet waste placed in a non-biodegradable plastic bag and thrown in the bin ends up in landfills. Also, raising animals for meat products to feed our cats and dogs carries a substantial carbon footprint.

Pets make an alarming contribution to global warming, as Professor Gregory Okin from UCLA university calculated. The meat-based food eaten by dogs and cats in America generates the equivalent of about 64 million tonnes of carbon dioxide per year – this has the same yearly impact on the climate impact as driving 13.6 million cars. Okin also found that cats and dogs are responsible for 25 to 30 per cent of the environmental impact of meat consumption in the United States.[44]

Make no mistake: I am not anti-dogs or anti-cats; it's not their fault. What's really concerning is the mindlessness of the human race to create the need for lives that do not belong and in plague proportions. This is what happens when it's all about the survival of the individual rather than the survival of the whole. Are our human relationships so inadequate that people need pets to fulfil their emotional needs, and to replace the inadequacies of a relationship with pets? If that is so, should we not be looking at the inadequacies in the way we relate to each other? What needs to change for us to become healthy humans who create healthy relationships with other humans?

Reflections to reflect on

- Save our wildlife from pets.
- Save our planet from pet shit.
- If your relationships are so inadequate that you need a pet then take a look at yourself and ask why?
- You have no right to be mindless – your only rights are to look after the planet and become a responsible inhabitant of this planet.
- Lose your self-important arrogance and be humbled by the magnificence of this planet we call home.

CHAPTER 12

THE MISSING LEG AND THE LOST WOMB

Is gendered behaviour reflected in the way we wee? Does it all come down to how we "PISS", urinate, take a leak? Isn't the basic primal need to pee what makes the first noticeable behavioural difference between girls and boys?

Males urinate upright, legs spread, extending themselves outwards. When males urinate their parameter is also extended, because they can project their pee giving them more manoeuvrability and choice of where to aim and where their pee lands. Men can choose to urinate deliberately on something just because they can. They often as adolescents will think it funny to be disrespectful to another creature by urinating on it. For example, on an ant's nest, a passing beetle. Are these not the often-dominant male traits of needing to lord over, needing power, wars, carelessness, lashing out, just to name a few generalised characteristics – do guns bare any phallic resemblance?

Another observation is that males have to know in which direction to urinate so as not to get wet. Is this where the myth that males are better at directions comes from?

Men are more susceptible to destruction without thought of consequence. In comparison females squat close to ground making themselves smaller, less manoeuvrable and their urine affects a smaller space. They must be more cautious about where they squat (not to pee on an ant's nest for example). Knowing wind direction isn't necessary being so close to the ground; considerate, reflective, vulnerable, self-deprecating just to name a few generalised characteristics.

Females are more vulnerable than males when pissing. Is this possibly why females are more susceptible to creating community, or being peace-loving and thoughtful to the consequences of their actions?

Is it time to become gender conscious of our actions rather than being in the "wee" unconsciousness?

Who came first, woman or man?

If women have the XX chromosome and males the XY, then Y is a mutation or a diminished version of X, making the male part 75 per cent female with a missing leg. Whereas the female is the pure and original species. She is the motherboard from which we are all created, and men are a created specimen coming from women. Therefore, man comes from woman, and she came first! Even the word man is an abbreviation of woman. No ribs exchanged here! Which means that if God created man in his image, then God must be a woman creating woman in her image and woman created man in her womb.

Let's take a look at the male Y and the female X chromosomes, from a different perspective. The Y looks like an X with a leg removed. Also, males physically and phenotypically speaking are female, and the penis and scrotum are modelled from the shape of the ovaries. For the first five to six weeks, all foetuses are female which means all males start as female and believe they are female. Contrary to the Adam and Eve fable that Eve came from Adam's rib, Adam in fact came from the original female.

The female starts with XX and males with XY chromosomes, making females the original blueprint while males are 75 per cent female and one-quarter male. When taking all that into consideration, one can only imagine the psychological and physiological trauma a male must undergo to survive not becoming female: he does that by releasing an inhibitor gene, called SRY, to push out one of the Xs and make room for the Y. The likely experience of a male foetus is that of an imposter, a suppressor of his internal female. He has ripped himself away from the original motherboard and this desperate will to succeed creates a propensity to compete and win. Does that sound familiar? It is not surprising therefore that males in general in this paradigm – if they are honest with themselves – often have an inherent hatred of women. They start with a deep feeling of needing to dominate for survival, even before birth, then once born from the womb (which they can never have) and let loose in a patriarchal culture, this can only lead to a diabolical situation not only for women but for men as well.

In a patriarchal culture, men find themselves feeling superior because after all, they were able to compete with and push into a female foetus and win. So, there is an inherent psychological unconsciousness of wanting to get as far away from being seen or thought of as female. The worst insult to a boy or man is to be called a "girl" or a "sissy" – for example, *"You throw the ball like a girl."* That inherent misogyny is then projected onto the mother, the original woman, and acted out upon all others of the same sex.

If we were able to liberate ourselves from the patriarchal paradigm and, from birth, start encouraging and allowing boys to express and experience their femininity (after all, they are mostly female with a "missing leg" and a lost womb), would we not get a less misogynistic culture in which women and men are free from the tyranny caused by men bred in a patriarchy? I know not all men are tyrannous but all men are bred to know they can be tyrannous and those who aren't, choose not to be for reasons as varied as those who don't question their own behaviour. I would like to add that in my observation, boys who grow up around women and girls are usually well-rounded humans who have learned to respect women.

Would women raised in a patriarchal culture allow their male children to express their femininity? Considering women are also born and bred in a patriarchy to be of service to men's macho egos for survival, do women know who they are outside this patriarchal culture? Are they able to separate the woman from the mother, the maid from the sexual object? What if this missing leg and lost womb gives males a sense that something is missing, and in and of themselves they are not complete? What if this manifests and is expressed through the penis (missing leg compensation), the phallus tool of power which dominates our culture? Men like to think they have an extra bit but in fact, they have an internal bit missing so they try to compensate with their penis. Perhaps the saying, "Men think with their penis" originates from the unconscious depth that resides in their biology.

What if the only way allowed by our culture to fulfil the need for connection to the motherboard is through the entrance we all came from, where experiencing the pleasure of reunion with the mother and the female happens? In other words, that experience becomes a major preoccupation and obsession in our culture.

Is the male penetrating sperm on a mission to its creator motherboard? Am I right in saying that until men find their femininity, women will never be at peace and neither will men?

Transitioning – The non-binary dilemma

Why am I not surprised that as gender roles start to relax, males want to express their true inner depth, which is originally female. However, for some, the male aspect of themselves isn't enough to express this and to live as a gender-non-conforming male. They also want to sexualise their body by altering it to look like a biological woman's body, stealing the biological woman's identity.

I have no problem with males needing to express their feminine aspect; however, what I do have a problem with is that they are not content with seeing themselves as a unique androgynous sex and something to be proud of. Even more concerning are the aggressive attacks on biologically born women who speak up on this issue. They are de-platformed and receive threatening attacks to the point of losing their right to have their say and the annihilation of their identity. As if women don't have enough misogyny to deal with in a patriarchy. The speed with which this is happening is alarming and is affecting women in sport and in all walks of life. Women are being discriminated against because a man in a dress is competing with them and taking spaces and opportunities away from them. Is this not another form of male oppression in the guise of a male's right to be a woman? Any violence that males in a dress commit, once they have declared their new gender, is becoming a statistic that is falsely attributed to biologically born women.

Is this not the ultimate in oppressive misogyny? What's worse is we are letting it happen because they are men!

AN APPEAL TO COMMON SENSE

Hey trans people, I admire your courage and I empathise with your predicament as I know only too well what it is like to live as a non-conforming woman in a patriarchy let alone a non-conforming man in a patriarchy. I implore you to stand up on your own and, yes, declare your need to express your femininity – after all, this is natural! Be

AN APPEAL TO COMMON SENSE

proud, call yourself a non-conforming man but please don't oppress biologically born women at the same time just because you can. That is misogyny at its worst! If you call yourself a non-conforming man or even a non-conforming-to-gender human, you will then be respected by all. No-one likes a bully!

See yourself as the new man, the man of the future renouncing patriarchy. Become a new kind of human to change the world – that's the best and most honourable thing anyone can do to change the stereotypes which oppress us all. If you wish for our culture to become non-binary, instead of confusing the issue with, "they and them" pronouns (once again a males' logic creating conflict and confusion), why not remove them altogether? There are many cultures that do not use pronouns in their language. It's not a new idea but possibly a more peaceful and sensible one.

You are in a good position to do this because you understand what it's like to be neither one nor the other. Don't be misguided by your ego, by thinking you can become a woman. Instead become the wonderful non-conforming-to-gender human, that you truly are, and that's how we will stop the stereotypes of gender. You are in a powerful position to do this so don't waste your time, energy and money trying to become women. Get real! A man can have feminine traits but can never be a woman. Let's all unite to create a new paradigm of non-gender conformity as a start to the demise of patriarchy and a life of equality.

The transgender issue has now become an industry and among others, the pharmaceutical companies are making a fortune! What if it was acceptable for men to wear dresses just like women wear pants and we lived in an egalitarian culture? Things surely would be less complicated, and no-one would be discriminated against for their choices. And what if we called our species "woman" instead of being known as "man"? After all, woman is an all-gender inclusive word whereas man is gender exclusive. We would speak of womankind instead of mankind! Something else we must work on as a culture.

In my observation, unlike trans women, trans men go about their normal life almost unnoticed without practising misandry nor trying to steal a biological man's identity.

Colour-blinding

Do the colours red and black shape our unconscious belief system and therefore our destiny? Christianity and its artists have made red the colour of the devil and of hell. We have been dressing girls in pink, a diluted version of the colour red, from birth; and the colour intensifies to red as girls become women. The red dress is a symbol of sexuality and prostitution – the "red-light" district, for example. As girls are we not conditioned to be sexual objects from birth? Who says colour isn't powerful?

According to Christianity, Eve was the first to sin and women all over the world have paid for this imaginary sin by enduring thousands of years of misogyny in not only their lives but their psychological development. "Only women bleed" and what colour is that evil blood of creation? So even with something as natural as menstruation, women are condemned. I wonder if violence is menstruation envy – a deep-rooted inadequacy from being born of and part of a woman yet without a womb? Generally, the only other way to bleed is to create violence or be the victim of violence – and who are the warmongers? Who are the major perpetrators of violence?

It is interesting that Christianity is a patriarchal-invented religion to gain power and control by making men superior, and what is the one thing superior men can't do? Give birth! To power over and be in control, one must oppress the thing one wants to control: the fact that only women give birth. I am not going to spell out the many ways women have been denied control of their bodies and the right to give or not give birth because they are too numerous. However, I will say one word: abortion.

I agree that women also take part in ostracising women because we have forgotten our past: herstory has been written and rewritten to favour the patriarchal system and we have all become his-story. From childhood, women are bombarded with misogynistic patriarchal values through advertising and social media, and with an expectation to serve. This is so relentless that misogyny becomes internalised to the point where women are unconsciously conscripted to oppress other women.

Here we are in the 21st century, after thousands of years of programming, indoctrination and brainwashing. Most of it has been through religion, and now advertising and social media continue to carry the misogyny flag and do a good job in continuing to divide the genders. Religion did it through witch hunts. Social media is the "witch hunt" of our time and takes no responsibility for the increase in self-harm and suicide rates among young women.

We are now all patriarchal, women and men, and we still believe the nonsense we have been fed to the point where misogyny is so rampant that even women don't realise it: they hate women and what's worse they hate themselves. Find one woman who likes her body or herself for that matter. In my experience, it is rare. Are we unconsciously, in our seemingly harmless traditions, causing psychological damage to our children by continuing to uphold these traditions and continuing to create generation upon generation of misogynistic cultures? Has our colour-blindness played a major role in creating a culture that accepts violence against our daughters and sons? Some will say, "My daughter loves pink and there's nothing I can do about it – she was born that way." Well, let's bring the collective unconscious into play. For those who don't know what that means, the idea was originally defined by psychoanalyst Carl Jung, who described it as "a collection of knowledge and imagery that every person is born with and is shared by all human beings due to ancestral experience". [45] How long have we, among many other gender-related issues, been colour-blind to the point where the collective unconscious becomes the norm and we do not realise it or question it?

Pink has also been used to identify homosexuals. It demasculinises, it feminises and it is considered unnatural.

Heterosexuality is not normal; it is just common and beaten into us from birth. Whereas if there were no taboos on sexuality, we would find a more balanced scale with some people at one end who prefer heterosexuality and some people at the other end who prefer homosexuality for men and lesbianism for women. The rest of the population would sit somewhere in between, creating a more flexible sexuality reliant on who enters one's life and the strength of feeling towards them regardless of gender or sex.

Boys wear blue. Blue, a dark enough colour to be almost black, is bestowed on boys from birth as a symbol of depth, power and authority: a light blue for infants and a darker blue as they age. Of course, we can't dress boys in black because symbolically it is the colour of death, evil and fear so we disguise black with the darkest primary colour. And as opposed to red, the brightest primary colour.

Let us not forget Disney, one of the most influential creators of stereotyping gender in children. Disney has made the colour black powerful, evil and something to fear and obey, and the colour white, pure and good. Not only are we as princesses dressed in white waiting for the tall, dark and handsome prince to take us to his castle in the sky, but the tall, dark and handsome prince must conquer and own the princess in white as she is an object of desire.

Something that concerns me in Australia is the use of the term "mate" by parents when referring to their male children. This term implies friendship and equality, and it would not be a concern if it was equally applied to girls. We also refer to male children as "little man" however we never refer to our female children as "little woman". Again, these are the seemingly small and innocent actions that form our psychology and divide genders.

Positive masculinity

As women, we have given part of ourselves to create the male of the species, yet in this culture among many things we have been denied our own masculinity. If we are to temper the present out of control toxic manifestation of masculinity we must as women reconnect with our own positive masculinity, put the feminine back into masculinity and masculinity back into the feminine, no "Viv la difference" here!

To reclaim our masculinity, we must have the courage to be bold, self-reliant, yet engage in community, have the self-respect to become unapologetic, become assertive but not aggressive and show leadership with mindfulness in all aspects of life. By integrating both the positive feminine and masculine within ourselves we can become the empowered women we were born to be, who are strong yet mindful and positive role models to future generations. Let's become women who dare to imagine ourselves not in the imagination of this toxic masculine paradigm full of patriarchal imagery and needs, but in the imagination with imagery of our own feminine paradigm, with the aim to create and manifest a more nurturing and unifying world for ourselves, our children and the planet.

Reflections to reflect on

- An example of positive masculinity is an empowered woman.
- Toxic masculinity is when the survival of the egoic prowess of manhood and masculinity becomes dominant and are at the expense and more important than the of survival of the whole. We are trapped in a marriage of polarities instead of the marriage of our own inner unity.
- If all instruments of war were shaped like a vulva, then a revolver would become a revulva and no-one would get hurt.
- If the only blood spilled is the menstrual blood of creation, the world will be at peace.
- I've often wondered if Australian indigenous people invented the boomerang in the image of a flaccid phallus. The indigenous men of central Australia performed penile subincision as a coming-of-age ritual, which meant they had to squat to urinate.
- A motherless child is a child without a planet.

Part 3
Bringing utopia into reality

CHAPTER 13

PERFECTION

In my observation, perfection exists when everything is in a harmonious relationship with its surroundings. Everything existing is of equal value. There is no ego in perfection for when everything is in balance, it survives and thrives without the need to compete or dominate. This can be seen in nature where everything has sat in balance for thousands of years and becomes out of balance when humans disrupt it by removing or adding. Perfection is constantly engaged with harmonious survival where everything is relied on to sustain and be sustained for a wholesome environment. When environments are tampered with, everything must compete to survive, threatening biodiversity.

When disrupted, the earth tries to re-establish balance and harmony through turbulence. It shakes things up and sifts through what exists to find a new balance until perfection is reached and everything stabilises again in a different way. Perfection has two faces: in order to maintain and renew existence, organic transformation is needed thus creating our misconception of life and death (good and evil). Perfection is not in the eye of the beholder – perfection just is! It becomes in the eye of the beholder when it is disrupted by factors that threaten, harm and overpower it. It then ceases to be recognised and harmony ceases to exist until possibly a new perfection can be reached.

When imperfection occurs, everything is in competition for survival and in constant need to power over. Power over is a human concept and when we stand in our own power, there is no need for power over anything. Therefore, power is not part of perfection. At present, the earth has been thrown so out of balance and has to try to rebalance at such a speed that the elements are – and will be – in constant turbulence until we stop and allow harmony to return. It will never be the same harmony but balance will be restored over time – but will the new balance sustain us?

Earth From Space (2012) and *Breaking Boundaries: The Science of Our Planet* (2021) are two excellent documentaries that I highly recommend. If they do not change your understanding and respect for our planet, then there is no hope.

What is aesthetic perfection?

I observe visual perfection when everything is in balance – nothing stands out to the eye until one focuses on one part of that perfection. Aesthetic perfection is where nothing dominates or is out of place and, depending on the attention it is given, moves in and out of focus equally, like zooming in and out. Artificial noises, like a motorbike or a lawnmower, don't move in and out but dominate even when one focuses on something else. Artificial noises make everything else disappear into the background and difficult to notice until the noise stops, while natural noises flow in and out.

Can perfection also exist in violence? The difference is that a lion will kill for survival whereas a human will also kill for pleasure or power. Therefore, unnecessary violence, which is not the same as violence for the sake of survival, is not part of harmonious perfection. Decay, on the other hand, is part of harmony because it rejuvenates for continual balance to occur and is part of perfection.

When we are in harmony with ourselves, we are in perfection; we are not at odds with anyone and one who is at odds with us isn't in balance. If we don't react mentally, physically or emotionally, but instead act in a considered and thoughtful and caring manner we stay in perfection.

PERFECTION IS SURVIVAL!

Perfection is the order of the universe.
    Serendipity is the communication of the universe.
        Matter is the creativity of the universe.
            Together all three make up the
                holy trinity which is the intelligence of the universe.

Reflections to reflect on

- What is perfection and does it exist?
- Is it an instrument of Gaia and is it divinity?
- Why do we strive for perfection? Is it because survival depends on it?
- Is perfection the fundamental modus operandi of the universe, the equilibrium that holds everything in an aesthetic balance and harmony for existence?
- Does everything moving harmoniously create peace?

CHAPTER 14

UNIVERSAL PRINCIPLES FOR SURVIVAL

For the sustainable survival of all that exists, living in harmony with the natural environment and only taking what one needs and giving back what one can, is paramount. Without this fundamental principle, which all must adhere to, there is no long-term survival – full stop. To live in harmony with the earth and each other, we need to adopt the following principles.

Respect
The natural environment is the hand that feeds, provides and sustains therefore, for long-term survival, respect for the animate and inanimate is vital. All creatures and creations are made from the same life-giving building blocks and must, at all times, be respected, appreciated and not taken for granted. The throwaway culture that we have created is the antithesis of sustainable survival.

Responsibility

We can act responsibly towards others and the environment by understanding the principles of cause and effect in every situation. We need to be considerate before acting unless reaction is absolutely necessary.

Cooperation

Working cooperatively with other humans and cooperatively caring for the natural environment will ensure that it continues to produce the necessities for sustainability. Our current notions of self-importance and self-righteousness lead to unhealthy individuals who endlessly believe that it is their right to do what they want and to take without consequence. A healthy individual considers the whole and acts in accordance with the universal principles for survival for the sustainable survival of all life.

Discipline

Having the discipline to not only regulate self-indulgence from a mental, emotional and physical perspective but also from a procreational perspective will result in a sustainable population for the long term. This will ensure the survival of our species and the other species we share the natural environment with. The current overpopulation of humans is unsustainable and the continuous destruction of the natural environment, to make room to feed and house the human population, is the way to the mass extinction of everything and everyone we share the planet with.

Community

Our current cultural model separates, divides, isolates and uses fear to control individuals by encouraging them to seek happiness outside of themselves, which as we know can never be long-lasting and constantly needs renewal. This makes humans vulnerable to becoming unconscious slaves to the powers that arise in these unhealthy cultures, powers who take advantage by profiting for their own gains and not for the greater good of a sustainable community or planet.

But what if we started living in healthy communities, made up of groups of people who have come together for a common purpose? These communities could be small or large, living together or near each other and sharing a common life. Living in healthy communities creates strong bonds and feelings of belonging and while not stagnant, they would be permanent. Each person in that community would become a valuable member and would have the support of the community throughout the ups and downs. In times of crisis, holding that community together for the greater good would become important for not only the health of the community but for the health of each individual in that community. A healthy community must also practise the universal principles for survival as outlined in this chapter.

Intuition, wisdom and thoughtful reflection

We must learn (or remember) how to use our intuition – it is the most prudent guidance for taking considered and considerate actions. We must also draw wisdom from past experiences to thoughtfully reflect on and adapt to changing circumstances before creating new ways to better ourselves and finding more efficient ways to live sustainably. We also need to have the courage and the willingness to adjust to social structures accordingly by acting to enhance what is appropriate for the greater good.

Patience, conformity, tolerance and humility

We need the humility to be patient and tolerant with ourselves and all that surrounds us. We must participate in necessary action for the greater good in every moment and not take things for granted. Taking things for granted leads to apathy, which in turn leads to judgement and ultimately poor behaviour, which does not serve the greater good.

Practical survival skills

The technological age has robbed us of our capacity to survive by our own means. It has deprived us of our basic survival skills through inbuilt obsolescence along with a takeaway, cheap-food culture and throw-away economy. The less we use our practical skills to create our everyday needs, the more dependent we become on the system to provide for us, the less empowered we become and the easier we are to be manipulated at the will of those in power. Once these skills are lost, they become difficult to regain.

Reducing the human population drastically and creating sustainable communities which comprise of smaller numbers of people is paramount to long-term sustainable survival. This is because each individual is integral to the community by contributing on all levels from emotional support through to the provision of food.

Humans are deluded to think being provided for is the ultimate success. We all want to be useful and feel that we belong, otherwise our mental health becomes a problem and low self-esteem, apathy and selfishness become common. Unfortunately, like everything in our culture, we don't fix the cause, but use Band-Aids such as anti-depressants and other medications we believe we need. These seep into the environment through urination and upset its balance and biodiversity.

Clear communication

To attain healthy communities, individuals need to be brave enough to speak honestly and caringly, stretch out of their comfort zone, tell difficult truths, ask difficult questions, listen and learn. Even though it may be challenging, clear communication is a kind offering of respect. It's a way of doing power differently and respectfully for the greater good.

Spirituality

In our Western culture, spirituality is thought to be part of religion or to only be religion. Spirituality is, in fact, the antithesis of religion. Religion is a patriarchal construct designed to control, oppress and manipulate the world and everyone and everything in it, with a vengeful male god at its helm in the guise of spirituality. On the contrary, spirituality is about the awareness of our connection to our inner self, the earth and the universe, because we are all made from the same molecular structure. When we break down that which we are made of, it becomes part of the universe. Spirituality is not a tool or vehicle for control or manipulation and is more akin to Eastern spiritual practices such as yoga and meditation, which are more feminine-centred.

To create a new form of spirituality, it would be prudent to marry two aspects: manifestation and being. But beware that all our religions today are patriarchal in principle even Buddhism. The ultimate in spirituality would be the ability to care, respect and be aware of, involved in, and with, all that surrounds us, yet without attachment. Non-attachment – meaning not letting your personal and often obsessive wants interfere with the process of life.

If there is no attachment, there is room for non-reactive reflection and replenishment, making the act of caring more meaningful. This type of spirituality is more sustainable, and it is considerate and less wasteful.

Threats to the universal principles for survival

There exist many threats to the fundamental universal principles for survival. Unfortunately, we are our own worst enemy and perhaps the greatest threat to our survival.

Humans have the ability to create and achieve unbelievable feats and because of that, we are the greatest threat to ourselves and that which surrounds us. Without the structure of the universal principles for survival, and the skills needed to sustain them, we are subject to losing perspective and susceptible to emotional and psychological indulgences such as those outlined below.

Boredom: The root of all evil, boredom is when a person's emotional and psychological state becomes unbalanced and they experience life as tedious and dull, showing no interest in their environment and their surroundings. This often leads to creating a varied and often destructive behavioural and antisocial pattern, which includes anything from depression and inaction to imprudent action and violence.

Self-indulgence and self-entitlement: These human afflictions often mistaken for individualism and rights, stem from boredom. Our culture trains us in creating the endless need to take without moderation and with a mindless, insatiable hunger to be entertained. This condition leads to a belief that one is entitled to these indulgences so humans end up manifesting destructive natures.

Fear: A "tried and true" tool for control and manipulation, most of the world currently lives in fear – fear of hunger, fear of violence and fear of death. Women have lived in fear of these threats for thousands of years and have come to accept this as the natural order, as part of life and as part of survival in the patriarchal world in which we live. Fearlessness is freedom – if one does not fear one cannot be controlled.

Other common destructive traits include:
- Apathy – lack of concern
- Wastefulness – carelessness
- Greed – selfish desires
- Arrogance – exaggerated self-importance
- Violence – intention to hurt
- Hatred – extreme dislike
- Power over – control of others
- Entertainment – needing to be constantly entertained
- Jealousy and envy – resentment of other's advantages
- Anger – annoyance at not getting one's way.

Reflections to reflect on

- Feel the fear and keep moving with awareness until you move through the fear, stay alert and trust your intuition to guide your reasoning.
- Be alarmed about everything – it is what keeps one vigilant and alert.
- Always be aware that the worst can happen and be pleasantly surprised when best happens.
- Sometimes things have to be shown in the black-and-white for them to be seen and understood to make a change.
- I can only shake my head in disbelief at how skilful men are at making a mess.

CHAPTER 15

THE IMPORTANCE OF GOOD GOVERNANCE

We need good governance if we are to survive and make the difficult decisions to apply the universal principles for survival. Our current governance, to put it mildly, is not good and may I add that good governance is not possible until there is unity. Unfortunately, our prohibitively huge population makes it difficult and even impossible to unite for a common purpose to allow for good governance.

In our current political systems, we are governed by the economically powerful or "power–fools" who encourage this self-indulgent, entitled behaviour through the media. The media, especially advertising and social media, is extremely powerful and an effective platform in securing the human need for self-indulgence. It is not only a platform of the powerful, it is also part of the powerful elite. Our leaders are no longer politicians with a calling to better humanity but are predominantly ego-driven, career-minded mostly men seeking to elevate themselves at the cost of humanity.

This system leads to an insatiable appetite to want. This appetite, without moderation, becomes an addictive drug that makes both the powerful and the powerless scrupleless in how they satisfy this insatiable appetite. They become like a ravenous monster, raping and pillaging resources until there are none left. Eventually it implodes, making survival in the long term untenable.

This system separates and divides, making it almost impossible to maintain or even achieve unity or community. The survival of the individual who is disconnected from the whole becomes an entity who believes they have the right to do anything no matter the consequences.

Areas that need immediate attention

We have reached a point in our world where we will not be capable of making the sacrifices needed to save ourselves. However, I will attempt to mention areas of concern where new solutions must be found and adopted for future survival.

- We need to look to our past and the indigenous peoples of each country to salvage and integrate the good from their cultures and ours.
- We need to find a new paradigm that is not testosterone-based because, at present, this makes our world more vulnerable to violence, corruption and disconnection from the environment.
- We must stop the production of plastic: clear the oceans of it and get NASA to stop being self-indulgent and deal with this problem instead of going to Mars.

- We urgently need to take control of the human population.
- We need to remove capitalism as a financial system and replace it with a system that does not create such enormous divisions between rich and poor.
- We need a system of government that is not dominated by men, by career politicians or by majority rule. It must be a system in which our leaders are people who are committed and passionate in their field. For example, the ministers in charge of portfolios should be people whose field of work is in the title of the portfolio.
- We need to look at and embrace the world as a whole and find solutions that will allow survival on the planet and of the planet.
- We must stop seeing climate change as a concept outside of ourselves and realise that we are the problem no matter where we look. We need to stop saying climate change and start saying, "human damage change".
- We must stop cutting down our forests NOW – trees are sacred!
- We must stop carving up the earth like it is not our home (good planets are hard to find!).
- We must place a yearly carbon allowance limit per person so that we each prioritise how it will be used.
- We must stop the endless building of housing, which is needed due to overpopulation and start living in communities that share space and resources.

- We must stop eating seafood for at least 10 years to save our oceans because without a healthy ocean, there is no survival on this earth.
- We need to implement the rationing of carbon emissions, food and resources. We did it for the war effort – why not for our home planet Earth?
- We need to limit the use of technology so that it becomes a tool for survival rather than a platform for manipulation.
- We must limit the use of alcohol – many people in our culture are functioning alcoholics and that is how we cope with the world around us. Alcohol acts as a mask or a veneer, making us think that we are coping but our world is breaking down around us. As long as we can drink ourselves stupid every evening, everything is okay. Alcohol affects the way we relate to ourselves, our families and so much more. Drink-driving is illegal and why is that? As long as we are not driving, we can drink as much as we like and most of our personal relationships are conducted under the influence of alcohol and that is acceptable?
- We must stop our pet obsession for the sake of the planet We should find and make meaningful connections with others of our species.

Testosterone-fuelled leadership

Men, as leaders, have a testosterone-based logic, making them more vulnerable to violence, corruption and disconnection from their environment. The male energy seeks power and control over others and to achieve this, it needs to create a social and financial structure of inequity, not only between women and men, but also in the way of a class system. It creates a race of women and men in servitude to do their dirty work at home and in their work. Testosterone is an aggressive sex hormone designed for survival in nature and, when taken out of context, applies negative masculine survival skills and attributes to an artificial world of men's own imagination and replaces the following:

- The skill of the hunt. This has been replaced with competitiveness to attain power with the use of violence, war, rape and pillaging, to separate, control and conquer.
- Strength. This has been replaced with aggression to dominate and control.
- Personal power. This has been replaced with a desire for power and to power over.
- Tenderness. This has been replaced with sexual exploitation, which includes rape and the trafficking of sex slaves. Rape is an effective action for reasserting power, domination and control.
- Wisdom. This has been replaced with immaturity, greed, exploitation and the revered attainment of youth. There is disregard for the wisdom of age.

- Playfulness. This has been replaced with insatiable materialism. This type of culture uses and plays with war and violence as a problem-solving solution. Creating fear to control is its modus operandi.

A megalomaniac and pathologically egotistic leadership are what we end up with under the testosterone-driven logic of governance. I am not saying that all men fit that description, however, all males benefit from this culture and it is the males who govern our world. As a result, we are in great peril environmentally and as a species.

Role of women in governance

Women have been under male dominance for 2000 years and have been reared to exist for male purposes, losing their identity, access to personal power, and connection with each other and the natural world. Women operate behind a mask and hide behind men, hence the saying: "Behind every great man there's a great woman." Who is the archetypal woman when not behind a veil? What are her true qualities when she loses her internalised misogyny?

For both women and men who believe in male supremacy, a woman's place is in the home, the kitchen and the bedroom, and men have the right to determine what happens to women's bodies, including establishing and upholding anti-abortion laws.[46]

A recent example in the USA of men playing a major role in determining a woman's right to choose is the shocking overruling in 2022 of Roe verses Wade that was passed in 1973 to legalise abortion for all women.

Dear people we are moving into the dark ages!

I have no other justification for the women who participated in the overruling of the bill, other than that they are so far entrenched in the Stockholm syndrome they have become delusional to think that the oppression of women through a vengeful misogynist God is something to celebrate. Wake up!

This decision will quite likely give precedence for this out-of-control culture to rethink all the other issues we have made progress on like gay rights just to name one.

The idea that a woman's body is not her own and a woman's way of looking at reality is not valued, means the possibility of the world becoming a more emotionally intelligent place is not taken seriously. This is so ingrained in our culture that most of us don't even realise we operate from an imposed and internalised patriarchy and believe we are free from it in the 21st century. Women are imposters in the patriarchy and are treated that way in their everyday lives.

It is in our DNA and in our deep subconscious that as a culture, we are still functioning under the idea that women were born second and were first to sin. For these reasons when women are in power, they hold back. Women, entering leadership roles at present, have to play the testosterone game to survive. They also emulate male behaviour because they have no other role model. To be able to create a new culture, women must be able to recognise their oppression, unite and help each other tap into the wisdom of an oestrogen-based culture. This undoubtedly would change the course of our present imploding fate.

Studies have shown that in universities, women talk about one-third as much in class as men because women still think, consciously or unconsciously, *I'm supposed to be quieter* or *I'm supposed to give space.* Their assumption usually is that there's something lacking in them, and that idea comes from thousands of years of being told there's something lacking in them. Women are so used to being manipulated that they easily become complicit.[47, 48]

Finding different approaches to power

Women must discover their personal power to reverse the pattern of being easily manipulated to make them complicit. To create a new system, men as well must discover personal power as opposed to being in power. Once both sexes can achieve that, a true marriage can occur where respect is shared by all regardless of deference. What would this marriage look like and what is personal power?

The big question is: what does a woman not reared and moulded to survive in a male-dominated culture look like? What are her skills and attributes?

Here are some female attributes and what they become under patriarchal rule:

- Gathering turns to materialism
- Strength becomes dependence
- Personal power becomes low self-esteem
- Tenderness turns to trading for sex
- Wisdom turns into the woman behind the man
- Playfulness turns into the need to shop
- Loving becomes possessive and jealous
- Intelligence – both intuitive and rational – becomes the belief of being dumb
- Practical turns into housewife/secretary
- Fierce turns into emotionally violent.

So, there it is. Can women do a better job? Until they find their true selves and stand in their power rather than be powered over, I am not confident that they can. But, if women don't have a go then we are up shit creek without a paddle!

What is the perfect leadership equation?

Until humans can find personal power, we will stay on the treadmill and nothing will change. In the end, under this system, women become more emotional and men become over rational. Yet emotions and rationality are basic survival skills and when balanced in each human, we create equality and personal power starts to emerge. Personal power is when we are not needy but personally fulfilled by our own doing and do not need to power over others.

Emotions play a part in the body's interpretations of the senses, helping us to make good sense of life without becoming attached to that emotion. A sensory person rather than an over-rational or over-emotional person is a person on their way to finding personal power.

Importance of emotions and rationality

Balanced emotions are our friends; they alert us when there's something wrong and they tell us when something feels good. They are the first and most vital response system of our body and without them, we would be lost. However, when emotions are unbalanced, we become like robots, easily manipulated because we lose our sense of knowing what we want and we instead rely on others' decisions about our lives. We become addicts without information from our senses. When that happens, we become more emotional, leading to feelings of anger and hate.

Rationality is another friend because it allows us to make sense of emotional messages and act according to the situation at hand. What happens when balanced emotions are denied, and the world becomes over "rational"? An over-rational culture loses perspective. It becomes reliant on and obsessed with facts, and the overuse of science to tell us what to think becomes dominant. Because very few can now think intuitively or for themselves, unless an external entity shows us proof that something exists then it doesn't. Alas, we not only lose sense of any healthy humanity but we become the ambassadors of what they wish us to believe. This often turns out to be either unhealthy or corrupted or even untrue.

Technology, the platform by which we are now ruled, disconnects us from ourselves and others. This leaves us emotionally needy so we turn materialism into a survival mechanism, which only benefits the capitalist patriarchal system. To what end? So, the very powerful have so much money and power they can go to Mars, the moon and goodness knows where else, without any regard for humans or the planet.

What is personal power?

Gaining personal power gives our life meaning and comes to us incrementally as we grow in maturity and understanding throughout our life. It is a lifelong pursuit of inner growth and purpose, which gives us the strength and confidence to live our lives fully not only in our outer but in our personal world with honesty and integrity.

As we grow in personal power our need for attachment and reaction to situations diminishes and we are then able to become the observer of our life rather than the mindless reactor, never being able to move beyond a certain point of personal development. With personal power we lose the need to be right which is an indication that one feels powerless. Instead, we allow life to evolve without spending time complaining, blaming others for our choices and always being aware of the role we have played in the situation we find ourselves in.

Be aware of the language that you use and also be aware of how you use it especially if it implies a victim mentality. Language is a very powerful tool of action and along with thought determines what we attract in life.

If we are not clear we become vulnerable and we attract unwanted situations which puts us further into reaction and further still from reaching personal power. Take responsibility and learn from these unwanted situations by practising loving restraint instead of attachment and victim mentality. See it as an opportunity to reflect, learn and bring us closer to personal power.

Over time we will find that we attract less and less of these situations. When we can reach the stage of handling life through love rather than reaction, we can then forgive ourselves and others and healing occurs.

Having personal power means that we have the confidence to put in place healthy boundaries. We are clear about our values and standards, which do not drain our life force. This gives us energy to be with the people we love without attachment, and to do the things we enjoy without burden.

Taking personal space

Learn to relax by taking time out for yourself in order to respect and protect your energy so that you are free to give to yourself and others from a genuine considered place. Learning to relax will also create inner peace and the ability to make good life decisions. Include some strategies to help with relaxation on a daily basis which is helpful in maintaining personal power and reducing the egoic chatter going on in our heads.

Live life through a stream of love consciousness rather than through guilt and emotional neediness which is what we mistake for love in our culture. Live and understand the natural world, as you are one and the same. Anything you do to the natural world ultimately comes back to you.

For women, it is a natural instinct to want to nurture this world, and a well-nurtured world is one guided by personal power rather than being in power.

Compromise and personal power

While "compromise" is often described as the settlement of differences agreed by mutual concession, in our culture, the definition of compromise is better defined by one person having to give in to another's wants and desires, and where is the mutual concession in that?

Women especially have come to accept that having to compromise is a fact of life, and we have become very good at it. This is because it seems easier to compromise as a quick-fix solution to gain peace and acceptance, however, in the end, this becomes a pattern of avoidance. We can spend the rest of our lives compromised, which has quite a different meaning, with definitions ranging from vulnerable and impaired, to weakened or flawed.

In the long run, compromise as a solution leads to unhappiness, resentment, anger and, ultimately, depletion of personal power. A compromise is never a healthy solution for the mind, body or soul – of oneself or of another. A compromise that makes us feel compromised is our alarm bell and being able to find solutions that make us feel good about ourselves is paramount to healthy self-relating. If we are not honestly relating with our own self, how can we honestly relate with someone else?

In a situation that needs negotiating, it is important to arrive at a solution that makes all parties happy. It takes courage and honesty to negotiate situations with mutually acceptable solutions – so we mustn't give in! There are also times when a solution is not possible, and a stalemate is reached. This is our signal to say to the other person: "This is your need, and as much as I care about you, you must find your own solution." If these situations are common in any relationship, including friendships, then we need to ask ourselves: Is this relationship for me?

It may be that the other person comes to a solution that makes us feel uncomfortable, which means it is not a solution either – not for a healthy relationship. Or the solution may partially involve us, but if we have that little voice saying I'll just get drawn in again if I agree, then again, it is not a solution. Until the solution makes us feel self-empowered rather than pressured into compromise, a solution has not been found and a compromise has not been made.

When it comes to compromise in the workplace, there is a difference: at work we are being paid to do a job and there are times when we have to take direction. However, if that direction makes us feel regularly compromised, we need to ask ourselves: Is my work situation right for me?

To master not being compromised, it is important to practise and get to know when we feel yes, no, or even maybe inside of us in any given situation. Yes, is the only answer we should entertain.

THE LIGHT TO INNER PEACE

When unsure it helps to sit down, close your eyes, quieten your thoughts, breathe through your nose with awareness, and deeply to start with, allowing the out breath to clear your thoughts. Keep your eyelids closed and follow your sight through your closed eyelids, you will notice that there is always light there, it can be faint, white, coloured, patterned or an image, and that is okay. That light is the window to your spirit, your guiding inner self. Focus on that light and what you see there, allow yourself to relax and lose yourself in that changing light, keep watching any images which may come up and enjoy the wonder of it. If any images or thoughts come up, which make you feel uncomfortable or fearful, keep breathing and turn that image or thought into the image of a flower of your creation – turn your attention to the centre of this flower and watch this flower radiate out until it takes up all your vision behind closed eyelids then enter into the peacefulness of that moment. In other words, you have transformed that fear into something else and of your liking. This is how we release ourselves and transform our fears because most fears are in our imagination and imposed on us by our culture. Do this exercise for a short time to start with if you like. This will allow space for your inner self to guide you, expose any fears and give you a better understanding of your situation. It is much easier to communicate with yourself in the quiet. Practise this anywhere and as often as possible. You will find over time that it is a quick check-in with yourself in situations of uncertainty. Sometimes allowing yourself to have a nap as well can often make things clearer and it can also give you a fresh perspective.

I prophesise and I question but do not profess to necessarily have the answers, and the following are suggestions that can work with further development. Simply by applying the universal principles for sustainable survival (described in Chapter 14) as the touchstone for decision-making, we would achieve good governance. And we may consider the application of the nonagon system I describe below. Also, perhaps the approach taken by Ecuador, where in 2008 the rights of Pachamama (nature) were recognised in the constitution, could be adopted for "humanising" rivers and mountains so they have a say in critical decisions.

A new system of government

The nonagon system of government is based on nine aspects that need to be addressed in governing an area, a community, a nation or even world governance. It is not led by male career-politicians, nor necessarily by majority rule. The nine areas of governance could be:

- Energy access
- Sustainable transport
- Education and sustainable population
- Health and wellbeing
- Environment and climate management
- Sustainable agriculture and food
- Culture including arts
- Equity in diversity
- Justice and the rights of everything that lives on Earth.

Science, technology, communication and research would cross all these areas.

- Each of these areas would have nine representatives, each elected by their community/country.
- The representatives would need to have demonstrated commitment to the fundamental universal principle for survival and have working experience and expertise in the area they represent.
- A representative from each area would be chosen by the others to make up another nine representatives, who would come together as the nine leading decision-makers. They would be of equal status.
- Decisions would be made by consensus unless there is urgency then a majority of six would take place.

In theory, the nine who govern would be equal in decision-making and would be advised by the nine representatives from each area. The nine leaders would consist of five women, including two elders, and four men, including two elders. They would be committed and passionate in their field, unlike career politicians. There could be an additional council of nine advisors elected from each region, who represent that region. They could comprise a mixture of women, men, elders and young people. When a decision is needed to be made about a specific issue which, let's say for example in education, then a temporary group of nine would be chosen, which would include children, to come up with suggestions.

People would live in small communities of no more than 90 and share resources. Buildings and housing would be limited to 10 per cent of the land mass. Food production would be localised and take no more than 20 per cent of the land mass, leaving 70 per cent to the natural world for its survival and ours.

Once we achieve the optimal population size of 2 billion, each country's land mass will determine the sustainable population size allocation. The total land mass of the earth is 510,072,000 square kilometres, affording the population of approximately 2 billion. If we divide 2 billion people into the total land mass of Earth, we get 0.255 square kilometres per person. The population of each country, regardless of arable land, would be allocated 0.255 square kilometres per person. For example, Australia has a total land mass of about 7.692 million square kilometres and would afford a population of 1.9 million people. Australia's population before colonisation was approximately 750,000.

The nonagon system in practice

To maintain sustainability, communities would be restricted in procreation and maintain the original land-mass-per-population equation.

- Women of that community would decide who could be the child bearers at any given time in accordance with the population equation.
- All men would have vasectomies unless they were the chosen breeders, as vasectomies are easily reversed

allowing a variety of men to become breeders at different times.
- Communities would consist of varying sexualities, be open and be accepting of the possibility that everyone is on a continuum. If everyone was on a sexual preference continuum without societal taboos, most people would find themselves wavering in sexuality according to who they meet. A smaller percentage would be at the extreme ends of the continuum.
- There would be no gender roles nor restrictions on who can do what. That would be according to interest and skill rather than gender.
- Children would be the responsibility of, and raised by, the community as a whole.
- There would be cross-community social events for the sharing of knowledge, gene pool, trades, etc.
- I like the idea that there could even be a gift economy developed, that would take a very highly evolved culture, but something to consider.
- Children would live in their birth mother's community and all men and women would be the uncles and aunties as well as the custodians of each child.
- The abusers of respect for all life – mineral, plant, animal or the inanimate – would be shown the consequences of their actions and asked to suggest their atonement. This would be considered and included to enhance the offender's life rather than punish. Abhorrent and unthinkable acts would be a death sentence.

We all need time to find and explore personal power and with very little child-rearing to attend to, this system would be an excellent opportunity to do this. When both women and men can unshackle themselves from the hold of our current system and find their personal power, we can come back together on equal terms to create a culture based on both feminine and masculine sensibility, which is in harmony with our true natures and the planet, our home. That would be a true union of equals and not a marriage of servitude for both women and men.

I believe that my ideas will work and expanding on them as we develop will take us to new levels of understanding.

My concern is that at present, most people are not conceptual. Instead, they are followers and they need someone to follow. This means that people, in general, will not take the initiative needed to make these changes; the egoic conqueror paradigm will continue to power over as usual and the whole damn treadmill cycle will remain. I do not have great hope for the human race. I don't think we have the maturity to do what's needed nor the strength and the willpower because most of us are sleepwalking and inebriated by alcohol.

Reflections to reflect on

- Good leaders stand out but not so much that it sets them apart.
- How do we create a world without the need to power over and dominate?
- If we have to lead governments by protesting to make them aware of changes needed, then they are not working and we need to change how we are governed.
- The real government is Gaia. Listen to her.
- We create a new world by imagining it and then living it.

CHAPTER 16

THE END COULD JUSTIFY THE MEANS

The paradigm we live in, at present fuelled by patriarchy and capitalism, encourages our ego which is delusional and susceptible to indulgence. It can be easily manipulated to believe that it is never happy and therefore develops an insatiable desire for constant gratification. The ego, like capitalism, has the same "survival logic". It wants so desperately to survive that it will do anything, no matter how destructive, to fulfil its perceived need for survival. In the end, it will even destroy itself in that pursuit, and that is the logic of the ego-driven paradigm we are in.

Our egoic tendencies are our animalistic survival mechanisms, which make us arrogant and believe that we have evolved into a species that is better than the other animals we share this planet with. So, let's start acting like the truly amazing animals we believe we are by taking control, so we are no longer like herd animals – led by and for the use of the few faceless ones who control this paradigm.

The ego makes us think that when things feel good they must be good for us, but they rarely are. The ego needs to be put back in its rightful place to create balanced humans. The ego is just one component of our personality that is responsible for our impulses and dealing with reality. It ensures that what it perceives as reality can be expressed in a manner acceptable in the world it perceives as real. The ego functions in both the conscious, preconscious and unconscious mind, so it is a tricky character to deal with!

We have lost our way and need to empower ourselves by no longer being under the powers who control us. We must move beyond our self-importance and start taking seriously our precariousness as a species and the damage we are causing the other species we share this planet with. We need to practise respect, thoughtful reflection and self-restraint, and learn not to succumb to the egoic urges telling us that we must have because it feels good. Instead, we must reflect on these urges and before acting, use our intelligence and common sense to make considered decisions to ensure our actions do not harm others or the planet.

With respect, thoughtful reflection and self-restraint, we must find the best possible solutions that are akin to the fundamental universal principles for sustainable survival outlined in this book. We can use some of these thoughts and ideas as a starting point. Let's dare to become the great respectful human beings that we are by becoming self-aware and recognising which are the wasteful and destructive demands of the ego because they are endless and relentless, and surely, we are more intelligent than that!

With awareness, respect and self-restraint, we can start to come back into balance with the other aspects of who we are, integrating mind, body and soul. When we reach this self-discipline is when we reach perfection in ourselves. Then we can start to create a new paradigm with humble integrity and respect for all that is.

As a species, we have produced some truly amazing human beings, not by one mother nor by one father, but all of us have played a part in our evolution to produce these truly amazing humans. Let's all become truly amazing by working on ourselves and with each other to evolve into the amazing humans we can become, capable of achieving wonders! We are all creative, so let's start using that creativity by making what we can from what we've already got rather than from buying more stuff. We can ask ourselves; *Do I really need this new dress?* Or whatever else our ego is telling us we must have. When we don't know how to make or do something ourselves, we can always ask a friend for advice or help. Let's move out of our wasteful egoic delusion that more stuff makes us happy. Let's stop saying, thinking and doing the same things over and over again by not acting like a herd animal.

Alcohol seems to act as a reward system at the end of the day for having coped and survived another day in the patriarchal paradigm. We need to regulate alcohol and minimise relating with our friends and loved ones in an inebriated state. Alcohol fuels the ego and can have perilous consequences for relating! Let's empower ourselves with new thinking, by becoming more informed.

The websites and books of interest listed at the back of this book lead to new thinking, and the questions I have posed in each chapter can be used for reflection and discussion with family and friends. We can each find our own solutions to the problems we are facing and going to face – so, act now. Let's walk out of our inebriated slumber and become alive again so we can take control of our future and ensure the planet's survival because we and this planet are worth saving. We are amazing!

For Gaia's sake!

It is no longer about what is good for humans but what is good for the planet. Let's ask ourselves: What am I doing right now for the good of the planet and our long-term survival as a species? What am I going to do to create change in my lifetime?

Here are some small actions we can take right now to make a difference. We can continue adding to this list by informing ourselves, not through the "news", but by being seekers of knowledge and awareness. Let's continue to ask questions and not accept the garbage we are continually subjected to.

- Stop watching the "news". Glance at it occasionally but don't make it habitual. Instead, seek out knowledge. I stopped watching the news 30 years ago and the fear I stored inside diminished considerably.
- When outdoors, wear appropriate clothes for the weather conditions. For example, at the beach, wear light cotton, long-sleeve loose clothing, which covers

most of the body, instead of wearing sunscreen – an environmental pollutant. Also, always carry a scarf. Scarves are the most versatile piece of clothing and aid in protection with weather changes.
- The general rule is loose light-coloured clothing in summer and tighter dark coloured clothing in winter.
- Never wear sunscreen. Even if they claim it is safe, it is just another pollutant. Cover up with sensible and appropriate clothing instead, swim or walk early or late in the day when the sun is at its mildest.
- To minimise the human impact on the environment from a carbon and food supply aspect, don't replace or get a new pet – adopt a human instead or do volunteer work to engage with others.
- Use less of everything, especially food and seafood. Wasting food is a crime. How often I see people with ginormous fridges full of food which will eventually be thrown out. We must only buy what we need.
- I'll say it again: let's stop eating seafood for at least 10 years.
- Stop buying synthetics and eliminate buying anything wrapped in plastic.
- Stop buying plastic toys as they are short-lived and will end up either in landfill or in the sea. Help children find better ways to play otherwise all you are teaching them is to live in a throwaway society where nothing has value.

- Stop buying clothes (there is no-one I know who needs more clothing).
- Source places other than supermarkets to buy food and support local providers even if it is a little more expensive. When the global economy falls (and if we continue on this trajectory, it will), what can be produced locally will be our saviour.
- Support our local economy now before it's too late.
- Anything we can consume less of benefits the survival of all and if nothing else, will prolong our imminent fate, hopefully for long enough to implement solutions based on wisdom rather than solutions based on desperation.
- Refrain from being a mindless tourist – the carbon emissions from flying alone should be enough to start us thinking about staying home.
- When replacing your car rather than replacing it with a petrol or hybrid car replace it with an electric car. This company www.goodcar.com is a good place to start. They source what you need mainly from Japan and the UK. The cars are second hand and are affordable. The quicker we do this the quicker the electric charging stations will appear.
- In Australia we seem to fear being injured by fallen branches from the lovely old native trees in our gardens and on our nature strips. We have no compassion for these amazing and majestic life-giving trees, which are part of the planet's oxygen cycle, CO_2 absorption systems and also home to

many other species. We just cut them down instead of investing in the planet's future by getting a professional to look after them and removing the necessary branches to make them safe. I hear people say, "Oh, but we are planting another tree to replace it". Dear friends, it takes 40 to 60 years to replace the benefits to the environment of an old tree – we don't have that sort of time to reverse the damage we have caused! Trees are sacred!
- Stop worshipping the male god above us which does not exist and start worshipping the ground beneath us because that does exist.

We are now in a catch-22 with capitalism because it is responsible for lulling us into the false belief that we can reproduce and use without a care, creating huge populations which need resources for survival. Capitalism is keeping this large, unsustainable population together for now and only for the short term. We need to be prepared because in these changing times, anything can happen – and does – like a tsunami or a pandemic or even an economic crash. And it can happen suddenly and all at once. We can prepare ourselves by:
- Making sure we are part of a strong, supportive community. These can also be created by getting involved in our local area. In my neighbourhood, we have a food-swap every month where we share a surplus of what we have grown or made. Those who don't grow food can make something to share instead.

- As well as the food swap, a few of us have formed a dry-food collective to reduce packaging by offering an alternative to buying from a supermarket. We operate a monthly community distribution of good quality dry foods like flour, grains, nuts and fruit, which we source and buy locally where possible. It is not for profit and has been operating for three years. We are successful because it is low-key and we believe in the importance of giving to our community while minimising our community's footprint. We also operate from a room in a community-owned building at virtually no cost to the collective. I believe it is also successful because it acts as a monthly community get-together, where lots of chatter and good cheer naturally happen.
- Starting a regular ethical discussion group with friends and neighbours to discuss these issues in that forum. Even though we may not have the same philosophies, the people in my neighbourhood are supportive and caring. This did not just happen; we created it over the last four years.
- Knowing and interacting with our neighbours is very important and can also be done in an apartment building. In a time of global crisis, these are the closest people to us physically. Imagine if access to the internet was not available.
- Being flexible, adaptable and aware in all situations. Instead of waiting for things to happen and becoming the unconscious victim of something we have all created, start preparing now.

Community support helps to overcome fear. When we are in fear mode due to a situation, we are more easily controlled and manipulated because we perceive we are going to lose something. We have created our predicament by being thoughtlessly complicit. Our culture has an unconscious likening to the "Klingons" in the *Star Trek* series who have a saying, "Today is a good day to die." I say, "Today is a very good day to live." So, let's live with awareness and consciousness for the survival of our humanity and this unique and wonderful planet we call home.

Reflections to reflect on

- Start to learn how to really relate with all kinds of people instead of relating from the seemingly safe place behind closed doors
- Humility isn't a lack of confidence; humility is to have the confidence and courage to be humble enough to trust your senses and intuition to inform your reasoning and act on them with awareness.
- If you don't understand beauty then it appears evil because you don't recognise it and see it as something unknown, and anything unknown is to be feared in our culture.
- Is the creation of men the part of a woman gone wrong? And how do we bring that bit of us that's gone wrong back into the fold to save our species because we are terrific and worth saving. The men we have created are powerful and lost and play with dangerous tools. Not a good mix for survival!
- We don't give reverence to the place where we place our feet.

CHAPTER 17

UTOPIA OF THE IMAGINATION

The basic unit of all matter is the atom, which is made up of many smaller pieces, known as subatomic particles. Every atom contains a central core called the nucleus, made of particles called protons, neutrons and electrons, which exist outside of the nucleus. Atoms are the basic building blocks of ordinary matter. They can join together to form molecules, which in turn form most of the objects around us, including us.

Quantum physics breaks down what we believe to be solid into the building blocks that make up every solid structure. These are the same building blocks that make up the universe. Quantum physics has found that when we observe something, it appears to materialise as reality but when we don't observe, these building blocks are everywhere in an identical wave formation, waiting to materialise into what we want to see or believe to be. This means that when we want to create, we bring a creative thought into focus and the waves of particles take the shape of our creative, visualised perception, causing the universal building blocks to form in such a way that they appear to be solid. Nothing is really solid because the building blocks never touch each other. There is space around each individual building block that we perceive as empty, but in my experience it is that perceived emptiness that holds the infinite power of the universe. That empty space is called consciousness and that consciousness is surrounded by the universal building blocks which are at the disposal of consciousness to create whatever it likes – only limited by imagination.

Because nothing, in reality, is solid and the building blocks are indestructible, the possibility for continuous creation is infinite, including the shape we and all other materialised things around us have taken. This means that we and everything in our world are made from the same building blocks and have materialised in this perceived world in different shapes according to our unique need for creative expression. Extinction is just perceived solidity returning to the fundamental universal building blocks to be reimagined and reshaped.

I am sure that when asked, every person would have a different idea of what utopia is for them.

Space, light energy and matter are the fundamental trinity of universal consciousness for creation.

Space is what gives room for all to exist, light energy provides the means with which to create and matter provides the material with which to create.

QUESTIONS TO PONDER

- Is imagination the doorway to utopia? What if we could imagine and create a new paradigm that looks nothing like the one we are in?
- What if at the end of this life, we become our imagination and we can transcend and become part of the intelligence that has the building blocks as its canvas?
- What would we create?
- Would we create a non-gendered species of equal strength and understanding? By non-gender, I mean neither female nor male in sex.
- Are we happy with the never-ending gender inequality?
- What form would this non-gendered species take? What would it look like? What would their attributes be?
- Would they be non-violent, respectful, wise, creative and sensitive? Would they be reflective, empathic or even empaths?
- Would they be inspired and energetic rather than aggressive and egotistical?
- Where would their natural environment be?
- What would be their purpose?
- Would they be creative and responsible with their creations?
- What would their challenges be?
- How would a non-gendered species procreate? Would they need to procreate? Would this species live in communities?
- Would it be a creative, peaceful egalitarian species, living without the threat of bodily harm or violence?

Reflections to reflect on

- Fear stops us from imagining and without imagination we are lost.
- Fear becomes an entity of restriction which paralyses into inaction.
- Fear is an internalised threat imposed by those who control us.
- Make fear your friend by not fearing it but using it to make you streetwise so that you are no longer on the treadmill of destruction and disfunction.
- Allow the light of love to fill you with the strength to take you to your heart.

CHAPTER 18

THIS IS YOUR CHAPTER

Einstein wisely said that we can't create the future from where we are now; we have to go to the future in our imagination in order to create it.

Now is a good time to reflect on, imagine and express your utopia. For that reason, I am leaving this chapter blank for you to fill in. Have fun!

Adieu, my friends and custodians of this land – it's so good to have been here with you today. I feel your warmth, I feel your peace, I feel your sadness and I feel your bliss, and at this point in time we have each other and that makes me smile.

Let's smile with joy together, for in days ahead or days gone by this smiley peaceful warmth we share will take us to a place of our imagination.

To create the new, in the loving light.

Follow Nicola here –
https://www.nicolasagegardner.com

Endnotes

Please note that at the time of publishing this book the website references below were operational and the content was in line with the author's ideas.

Chapter 2

1. Turner, L. (2017, March 3). 6 modern societies where women rule. *Mental Floss*. https://www.mentalfloss.com/article/31274/6-modern-societies-where-women-literally-rule [Accessed 5 May 2022].

2. The Church of the Goddess Geo-Gaia. n.d. War on women. *The Church of the Goddess Geo-Gaia*. http://www.churchofthegoddess.org/war-on-women [Accessed 5 May 2022].

3. Dworkin, A. (1976) *Our Blood: Prophecies and Discourses on Sexual Politics*. Perigee Books.

4. Muller, C. & Sanderson, S. (2020, August 10). Witch hunts: A global problem in the 21st century. DW.COM. https://www.dw.com/en/witch-hunts-a-global-problem-in-the-21st-century/a-54495289 [Accessed 5 May 2022].

5. National Center for Victims of Crime. n.d. Sexual Assault Victimization. *National Center for Victims of Crime*. https://www.ncjrs.gov/ovc_archives/reports/help_series/pdftxt/sexualassaultvictimization.pdf [Accessed 5 May 2022].

6 Our Watch. (2018). Quick facts. *Our Watch.* https://www.ourwatch.org.au/quick-facts/ [Accessed 5 May 2022].

7 Anitha, S. & Pearson, R. (2013). Post World War II: 1946-1970. *Striking Women.* https://www.striking- women.org/module/women-and-work/post-world-war-ii-1946-1970 [Accessed 7 May 2022].

8 PBS. n.d. Women and work after World War II. *PBS.* https://www.pbs.org/wgbh/americanexperience/features/tupperware-work/ [Accessed 13 June 2022].

9 Churchill, L.B. n.d. The Feminine Mystique. *Britannica.* https://www.britannica.com/topic/The-Feminine-Mystique [Accessed 3 May 2022].

10 Donner, F. (1992). *Being-In-Dreaming: An Initiation Into the Sorcerers' World.* 1st ed. HarperCollins.

Chapter 3

11 Summers, A., 2016. *Damned Whores and God's Police.* 5th ed. University of New South Wales Press.

12 Parry, E. (2018, October 5). Love machine: We interview Harmony — the sex robot with a Scottish accent who likes threesomes. *The Sun.* https://www.thesun.co.uk/fabulous/5022057/interview-harmony-sex-robot/ [Accessed 7 May 2022].

13 Khadem, N. (2022, July 29). Sexual assault reports in Australia hit all-time high: What is driving the increase? *ABC News.* https://www.abc.net.au/news/2022-07-29/sexual-assaults-australia-record-high/101281802 [Accessed 12 Sept 2022].

14   IVF future. (2010, October 3). *Egg collection in IVF flushing follicels with a single lumen needle*. [Video]. YouTube. <https://www.youtube.com/watch?v=LD4HXwu8hgk> [Accessed 11 May 2022].

Chapter 4

15   Hopkins, D. (2021, March 2). The secretive world of Australia's arms exports. *Overland Literary Journal*. https://overland.org.au/2021/03/the-secretive-world-of-australias-arms-exports/ [Accessed 11 May 2022].

16   Keyes. C. (1966, October). "Suppose they gave a war and no one came". *McCall's*. https://www.genekeyes.com/CHET/Chet-1.html [Accessed 11 May 2022].

17   Green, J.M. (2021, October 21). What is stock market manipulation? *The Balance*. https://www.thebalance.com/stock-market-manipulation-5184361 [Accessed 11 May 2022].

Chapter 5

18   Bark. (2021). Bark's 2021 Annual Report. *Bark*. https://www.bark.us/annual-report-2021/ [Accessed 12 Sept 2022].

19   Brigham Young University. (2021, February 9). 10-year study shows elevated suicide risk from excess social media time for teen girls. *Newswise*. https://www.newswise.com/articles/10-year-study-shows-elevated-suicide-risk-from-excess-social-media-time-for-teen-girls?channel= [Accessed 11 May 2022].

Chapter 6

20   Revell, L. (2021, October 21). Microplastics are in the air we breathe and in Earth's atmosphere, and they affect the climate.

The Conversation. https://theconversation.com/microplastics-are-in-the-air-we-breathe-and-in-earths-atmosphere-and-they-affect-the-climate-170093 [Accessed 14 June 2022].

[21] Ocean Conservancy. (n.d.) Fighting for Trash Free Seas. Ocean Conservancy. https://oceanconservancy.org/trash-free-seas/plastics-in-the-ocean/ [Accessed 30 September 2022].

Chapter 7

[22] Agarwal, P. (2022, February 2). Malthusian theory of population. *Intelligent Economist.* https://www.intelligenteconomist.com/malthusian-theory/ [Accessed 11 May 2022].

[23] Suzuki, D. (2011, November 1). Overconsumption, not overpopulation, is the biggest problem. *The Georgia Straight.* https://www.straight.com/news/david-suzuki-overconsumption-not-overpopulation-biggest-problem [Accessed 6 May 2022].

[24] Wilson, E. (2003). *The Future of Life.* Vintage Books.

[25] Ritchie, H. & Roser, M. (2021). Forests and Deforestation. *Our World In Data.* https://ourworldindata.org/deforestation [Accessed 13 Sept 2022].

[26] Zimmer, K. (2019, November 23). Deforestation is leading to more infectious disease in humans. *National Geographic.* https://www.nationalgeographic.com/science/article/deforestation-leading-to-more-infectious-diseases-in-humans [Accessed 13 Sept 2022].

[27] Mulhern, O. (2021, May 24). Deforestation Simplified: Its the Food. *Earth.Org.* https://earth.org/data_visualization/deforestation-simplified-its-the-food [Accessed 13 Sept 2022].

ENDNOTES

28 DeNoon, D. (2006, November 2). Salt-Water Fish Extinction Seen By 2048. *CBS News*. https://www.cbsnews.com/news/salt-water-fish-extinction-seen-by-2048/ [Accessed 11 May 2022].

29 Stanford Report. (2006, November 2). *Science* study predicts collapse of all seafood fisheries by 2050. *Stanford News*. https://news.stanford.edu/news/2006/november8/ocean-110806.html [Accessed 13 Sept 2022].

30 Wolchover, N. (2011, June 1). When Will the Earth Run Out of Food? *Live Science*. https://www.livescience.com/33311-food-prices-global-hunger-skyrocket-2030-oxfam-warns.html [Accessed 13 Sept 2022].

31 Roser, M., Ritchie, H. & Ortiz-Ospina, E. (2019, May). World Population Growth. *Our World in Data*. https://ourworldindata.org/world-population-growth [Accessed 13 Sept 2022].

Chapter 8

32 Williams, M. (2014, December 2). What percent of the Earth is water? *Phys Org*. https://phys.org/news/2014-12-percent-earth.html [Accessed 13 Sept 2022].

33 Aende, A., Gardy, J., & Hassanpour, A. (2020). Seawater Desalination: A Review of Forward Osmosis Technique, Its Challenges, and Future Prospects. *Processes*. 8(8)901. https://www.mdpi.com/2227-9717/8/8/901

34 Science Blog. (2008, November 17). Water Vapor Confirmed As Major Player In Climate Change. *Science Blog*. https://scienceblog.com/17805/water-vapor-confirmed-as-major-player-in-climate-change/ [Accessed 1 May 2022].

35. McCosker, M. (2022, August 17). Across outback Queensland, Great Artesian Basin water is surfacing where it has never been seen before. *ABC News*. https://www.abc.net.au/news/rural/2022-08-17/emerging-springs-across-queenslands-great-artesian-basin/101260220 [Accessed 1 May 2022].

36. Water Source. (2019, April 10). Foreign ownership of water assets revealed. *Australian Water Association*. https://www.awa.asn.au/resources/latest-news/business/assets-and-operations/foreign-ownership-of-water-assets-revealed [Accessed 11 May 2022].

37. Aboriginal and Torres Strait Islander Social Justice Commissioner. (2008). 2008 Native Title Report. *Australian Human Rights Commission*. https://humanrights.gov.au/sites/default/files/content/social_justice/nt_report/ntreport08/pdf/chap6.pdf [Accessed 11 May 2022].

38. Saner, E. (2021, August 6). Lotion in the ocean: is your sunscreen killing the sea? *The Guardian*. https://www.theguardian.com/environment/2021/aug/06/lotion-in-the-ocean-is-your-sunscreen-killing-the-sea [Accessed 13 Sept 2022].

Chapter 9

39. World Health Organization. (2021 March 9). Devastatingly pervasive: 1 in 3 women globally experience violence. *World Health Organization*. https://www.who.int/news/item/09-03-2021-devastatingly-pervasive-1-in-3-women-globally-experience-violence [Accessed 13 Sept 2022].

40. World Vision. n.d. Child Abuse: Facts, Stories & FAQs. *World Vision Australia*. https://www.worldvision.com.au/child-abuse [Accessed 9 May 2022].

Chapter 11

41 RSPCA. (2020, March 6). How many pets are there in Australia? *RSPCA Knowledge Base.* https://kb.rspca.org.au/knowledge-base/how-many-pets-are-there-in-australia/ [Accessed 13 Sept 2022].

42 Ham, A. (2017, March 17). Australia's Cats Kill Two Billion Animals Annually. Here's How the Government Is Responding to the Crisis. *Smithsonian Magazine.* https://www.smithsonianmag.com/science-nature/australias-cats-kill-two-billion-animals-annually-180977235/ [Accessed 12 May 2022].

43 Holderness-Roddam, B. (2011). *The effects of domestic dogs (Canis familiaris) as a disturbance agent on the natural environment.* [Research Master thesis, University of Tasmania] Open Access Repository. https://eprints.utas.edu.au/12310/ [Accessed 13 Sept 2022].

44 Hewitt, A. (2017, August 2). The truth about cats' and dogs' environmental impact. *UCLA Newsroom.*

https://newsroom.ucla.edu/releases/the-truth-about-cats-and-dogs-environmental-impact [Accessed 3 May 2022].

Chapter 12

45 Fritscher, L. (2022, March 18). What is the Collective Unconscious? *Very Well Mind* https://www.verywellmind.com/what-is-the-collective-unconscious-2671571 [Accessed 30 Sept 2022].

Chapter 15

46 Penny, L. (2019, May 18). The criminalization of women's bodies is all about conservative male power. *The New Republic.* https://

newrepublic.com/article/153942/criminalization-womens-bodies-conservative-male-power [Accessed 14 May 2022].

47 Jule, A. (2004). *Gender, Participation and Silence in the Language Classroom.* 1st ed. Palgrave Macmillan.

48 Trinity Western University. (2004, June 21). Boys speak up, girls silenced in the classroom. *Newswise.* https://www.newswise.com/articles/boys-speak-up-girls-silenced-in-the-classroom [Accessed 15 May 2022].

Additional Books of Interest

Jane Goodall and Douglas Abrahams (2021) *The Book of Hope: A Survival Guide for an Endangered Planet.* Penguin Random House, UK.

James Nestor (2020) *Breath: The New Science of a Lost Art.* Penguin Random House, UK.

Jennifer Cameron (2021) *Ancient Ways for Current Days.* Ultimate World Publishing, Australia.

Dorothy Bryant (1976) *The Kin of Ata are Waiting for You.* Random House, USA.

Eckhart Tolle (2004) *The Power of Now.* Namaste Publishing, Canada

Germaine Greer (1970) *The Female Eunuch.* Granada Publishing Limited, USA

*An interesting organisation to join for personal growth and spiritual awakening is Sounds True, a multimedia publisher of books, audios, podcasts, online courses, certification programs and music.

Notes

www.ingramcontent.com/pod-product-compliance
Lightning Source LLC
Chambersburg PA
CBHW041139110526
44590CB00027B/4075